OTHER BOOKS BY HAL BORLAND

The Outdoors

AN AMERICAN YEAR
THE ENDURING PATTERN
BEYOND YOUR DOORSTEP
SUNDIAL OF THE SEASONS
COUNTRYMAN: A SUMMARY OF BELIEF
OUR NATURAL WORLD (EDITOR)
HILL COUNTRY HARVEST

People and Places

THIS HILL, THIS VALLEY
HIGH, WIDE AND LONESOME
THE DOG WHO CAME TO STAY

Fiction

THE SEVENTH WINTER
THE AMULET
WHEN THE LEGENDS DIE
KING OF SQUAW MOUNTAIN

Folklore

ROCKY MOUNTAIN TIPI TALES
THE YOUNGEST SHEPHERD

Poetry

AMERICA IS AMERICANS

HAL BORLAND

Homeland

A Report from the Country

J. B. LIPPINCOTT COMPANY
PHILADELPHIA AND NEW YORK

First edition.

Printed in the United States of America.
Library of Congress Catalog Card Number 69–16166.

Designed by Dan Walden

for Barbara —

When I must leave, I pray it will be May,
For I'd remember earthly things this way:
An apple tree in bloom, the breath of dawn,
An oriole's ecstasy, a dappled fawn,
A whippoorwill at dusk. I would hereafter
Remember now in terms of your sweet
laughter.

FOREWORD

I ONCE SAID that because I live where I do and write as I do, I felt like a foreign correspondent reporting an alien scene. Now, as I go over the material in this book, I feel more like a native sending dispatches to a foreign place. I even have the uneasy feeling that I might need a visa to visit the cities where my reports are read. For these are the reports of a rather leisurely countryman that are sent out periodically to an urbanized, technically-oriented world so clock-hounded that even its occasional leisure is taken in haste. And in a time when so much of humanity seems obsessed with impermanence and rootlessness, I have been writing about a way of thought and life that is both literally and figuratively firmly rooted in the soil of this earth.

Also, this book is a kind of anachronistic adventure because in it I am attempting to slow down time instead of speeding it up. It covers five years of my life, which in a way should make it autobiographical. But instead of telling what I was doing day by day or even week by week, I dip into those years only at three-month intervals and examine what I was thinking. These dippings are in sequence, but they largely coincide with the big, deliberate rhythms of this planet, the solstices and the equinoxes.

Such a plan, of course, is completely out of phase with current trends, which demand immediate answers and opinions. *If a computer can give us an answer in a fraction of a second, why does a man need an hour? or a day? or three months, for God's sake!* Well, to give an immediate answer to that I would say, first, a man isn't a computer and, secondly, a computer doesn't have any thoughts, ideas or opinions. All a computer can do is follow through on a programmed question, which means a code devised by man, and give factual answers that have to be decoded. So please, let's not confuse the machines with those who invented them and are supposed to run them. Let's keep the identities straight.

That is another pertinent point—identity. Time is not only relative, but its dimensions vary with those affected by it. My time is totally different from that of a May fly, say, which lives three or four days at most, usually only a few hours. There is the time of the summer insects—fireflies, June bugs, crickets, katydids—which hatch from the egg in early summer and perish, at the latest, with the first hard frost. There is the time of the dooryard robin and the chickadee at the winter feeder, which are fortunate if they live five years. A bullfrog may, with luck, live fifteen years, a horse twenty, a grizzly bear twenty-five. But I, being a white human male animal, have a total life expectancy of about eighty years. Because of my own identity, then, time has a particular dimension for me. During my lifetime I probably shall know 320 three-month seasons, each of which equals the total lifetime of a summer insect. When I take twenty such seasons, as I do in this book, I am taking only a small fraction of my total experience.

But the time factor did shape this book and gives it a degree of meaning. The chapters were written as dispatches in the same order that they have in the book, and the sequence covers the past five years, an eventful time indeed. They were written originally because Morris Rubin, who edits *The Progressive,* a monthly journal of opinion, suggested some years ago that my country-based, nonpolitical viewpoint might be an offbeat addition to his magazine, which is primarily political and societal in its approach. But I wondered, and so did he, whether his readers could digest or successfully ignore my essays more often than quarterly. So we set them up that way, and I have been writing those pieces every three months since 1957. For this book I have chosen only those for the years since 1963.

I had thought I might have to rewrite major portions of these pieces to keep them from seeming hopelessly dated. When I read them over, however, I found little that I felt needed changing. The conclusions reached at the time still seemed valid. I am sure this can be interpreted either of two ways: either I had a fair degree of proportion and perspective, or I had nothing to say that was worthy of reappraisal. I prefer to think that the beliefs and findings were, and still are, rooted in persistent natural truth and fundamental reality that, like grass and trees and running water, are an enduring part of the earth itself.

I feel that though these past five years have been years of crucial events and decisions in the affairs of humanity, these dispatches add up to a statement of affirmation. At one point in them is this statement:

"What can a man believe in? I suppose it depends on what a man is looking for, but I know that if you watch a nesting bird and experience a midsummer dawn you can't fail to believe in something. In life and time, if nothing else. Given those, almost anything is possible that a rational man might want."

That, to me, is the key. This book represents a search for the substance of a belief that will satisfy the questing mind of a rational man. I have found it in a nesting bird, a midsummer dawn, a winter snowstorm, and a great many other things seen and heard and felt, and to some degree understood, from here in my rural dooryard and out in the meadows and up on the wooded mountainside. That really is what these dispatches are all about.

H. B.
Salisbury, Conn.
1969

Contents

HOMELAND

A REPORT FROM THE COUNTRY

1964—SPRING

April and the Challenge

It WAS a rough winter and I thought I heard the hills heave a sigh of relief when, at last, it began to break up. I know there was a whisper among the pines and hemlocks on my mountainside the evening the spring peepers began to yelp. And I never heard a more satisfying chuckle than that of the brook in the back pasture when it really warmed up and the melt began surging down to take out the ice that had locked the brook in silence for weeks on end. We even welcomed March's cold mud and gusty wind.

Maybe it was not the high-level bomb testing that snowed us in and froze us stiff—the Weather Bureau insisted it wasn't, though the best explanation the Bureau's spokesman could come up with was that "these things happen." But I'll lay odds that it was not the fault of the squirrels or the woolly bear caterpillars, either. Whether nuclear testing was responsible or not, I think the Weather Bureau should go along with the rest of us who say, "Stop it," just in case. It certainly is a factor in the emotional, philosophic, and political weather with which all of us have to live.

But that, like so many other matters affecting not only my health and comfort but my very life, seems to be out of my hands. Somewhere along the line I unwittingly delegated, or somebody delegated for me, that and too many other responsibilities and decisions. About all that is left for my hands to do, now that there are visible signs of the vernal urgency, is to clean up the winter's untidy litter and prepare to co-operate with spring and the compulsions of growth. I have been doing just that.

After a winter of relatively light physical activity I am always annoyed at how unwilling are my muscles and sinews to exert themselves. I think those alarmists who insist that a snow shovel is as lethal as a firearm are being egged on by the manufacturers of snowblowers. Last year a man I know took their warnings to heart, refused to touch a snow shovel and tramped out paths through the drifts to his garage and mailbox. He made out till the January thaw, when all the snow melted except what he had tramped down, and he fell on the ice right in front of his own door and cracked a wrist, broke a fibula and got a concussion and a head gash that needed ten stitches to close. Last fall, back on his feet again, he got out the snow shovel the minute he saw three flakes drifting earthward. "I'd *rather* die of a heart attack," he told his doctor, defiantly. "It's quicker."

I shovel snow, in moderation and taking my time, but my slack muscles still complain when I start the spring clean-up. But I have been picking up the dead wood the storms brought down and trying to bring order out of the natural clutter. Out in the yard the other day it occurred to me that nature does not bother to clean up and set things in what man considers proper order. Nature is not very tidy. It thrives on litter and unfinished business, as I cannot fail to see every time I go up into the woodland. Without the fertility of its own past, nature produces scrawny growth. Even with it, nature takes its own time. Only man wants everything tidied up in neat packages and disposed of now, today.

That tendency seems to have grown upon us. We want instant everything, from coffee to calculations, from cake to cures. We have achieved instant devastation, so now we must achieve instant antidevastation. If instant decisions go wrong, that is going to be just too bad; but there won't be many left to question. Probably not much of anything will be left except the trees and the insects, trees in remote valleys and insects in the ground. Insects and trees don't ask questions. They will go right on, deliberate as always, and start to repopulate the earth.

Raking litter and carrying dead branches to the brush pile, I thought of the way this land was cleared and possessed to begin with. The land itself was the challenge, and that challenge made men strong in body and spirit. True, it broke some men, and it was an unbearable trial for many women. But it did breed a stout, resolute race. Life is easier today, physically easier at least. But was ease the goal? Not really. If it had been, this country would still be a prosperous fringe of colonies along the Atlantic seaboard and an equally prosperous margin of ranchos and missions along the Pacific shore.

The challenge has led the way as far back as we can trace our own beginnings. Biologically speaking, man's remote and primitive ancestors faced the challenge of survival in a world dominated by giant reptiles. An evolving brain equipped man with wit and wisdom to meet the challenge of fang and claw. Once up on his hind legs and armed with fire and a stone axe, he accepted the challenge of his habitat.

The long story of civilizations is a repetitious chronicle of challenges met, mastered, and followed by periods of ease. Ease begot weakness, and new tribes still facing the challenge rose to dominance. One of the oldest stories we know, one that keeps repeating itself, is that of the conquest of effete cultures by hungry hordes of rude outlanders, barbarians.

Two basic challenges have persisted for man throughout history. Others come and go, but the challenge of the weather and the challenge of the land are basic to every chapter in man's long adventure. Man has had to shelter himself against the storm and cold, and he has had to find the food to assuage his hunger among the plants and animals native to this earth, his habitat. He has thriven, as an individual and as a society, in direct proportion to his success in managing those necessities—in staving off frostbite, sunstroke, starvation and thirst. And his civilizations have risen or fallen with their available supplies of food, water and raw materials, all of which come from the land.

With that in mind, I wonder why there is such a note of satisfaction in the periodic announcements of new statistics showing a further decrease in the area of our farmland and other open space, and a further reduction of the population still living on the land. And I have been wondering why all of us except the ski crowd resented the rigors of this past winter's weather. The answer to that question is easy. Nobody in his right mind likes to live half-frozen in the middle of a perpetual snowdrift, and nobody claps hands at the sight of his January and February fuel bills. The other answer is a bit more involved.

Being a countryman by choice, I have certain biases in favor of the country. I moved here because I wanted to, and I stay here because it provides a good way of life in a place where I can make a living. So perhaps I see things in a different light than a noncountryman. I believe that the country—the uncultivated land and the remaining remnants of wilderness as well as the farmland—is essential to the whole nation's sense of proportion and its perspective. It represents elbowroom, proves that there are still places on earth where a man can stretch his arms and legs and maybe even his mind. It represents a kind of freedom, personal freedom, that is not too common a commodity any more: freedom from mechanical din, freedom from crowds, freedom from mass mores and opinions. It represents such minor but important freedoms as the right to wear old clothes or drive a car more than two years old without worrying about social status, the right to sit and think, or just to sit, and not be labeled antisocial or neurotic.

Beyond affording such minor but humanizing personal freedoms, this nation's farmlands and forest areas are invaluable not only for the food they produce and the raw materials they represent but for their venerable and enduring challenge. They are ruled by the weather and the seasons and they partake of the big, eternal rhythms. They refuse to produce instant crops. The land demands of man a degree of patience and deliberation. It represents, if you will, an object lesson of that still unrepealed law of cause and effect, planting and harvest, work and reward. Winter passes and spring comes in their own time, and neither push buttons nor whirring wheels open the buds, bring back the migrant birds, set live water to flowing, and reawaken the soil.

These matters are impossible to see and live with and experience without having some glimmer of confidence in a persistent order and meaning not dependent on the guiding hand of man. I find that a welcome reassurance at any winter's end. Or any day's end, for that matter, summer or winter, spring or fall.

Feeling the grass and the slowly warming earth beneath my feet as I raked, I glanced out across the home pasture and up at the woodland on the mountainside. And I wondered why, as a nation and a government dominant in world affairs, we think it wise and important to do some of the things we do in the name of foreign aid. I keep hearing it said that we must help the underdeveloped areas to make a swift transition from penury to plenty, from primitivism to industrial prosperity, from an ox-age past to a jet-age present. On the face of it, who can argue with such a purpose? Forget for the moment, if you can, the instances when our material help has been in the form of guns and tanks and planes rather than plows and textbooks and medicines—freedom and democracy, at all costs, must be maintained, mustn't they? But sometimes it seems that we forget the importance of challenge and the necessity of growth. Sound nations as well as sturdy trees need roots in the litter of their own past. Times change and conditions alter, but not always or everywhere with the speed of the splitting atom. We have tried without notable success to produce instant nations. It may be that it can't be done, or shouldn't be. A steel mill, a power dam, even an ambassador to the United Nations, may be vital necessities to a modern nation, but not one of them is a germinal seed, really.

The land remains the essential challenge, anywhere on earth. It is man's environment, no matter where he lives, the essential factor behind every city and every suburb. Not even the computers can get around that, not even the orbiting satellites. Here it is, an indisputable fact, as real as my own pastures and the woodland beyond. And every April it reasserts its reality—torture and contort and abuse it as we may. Grass is green again and robins are singing on the margins of the superhighways, whether we see and hear them or not. The sun, not a law passed in Washington, melted the ice in the polluted rivers. Not even a *capias utlagatum* could keep a flood-swollen river out of river-bottom cities and farmlands.

And here in this rocky corner of the nation, where men named Hiram and Ebenezer and Adam and women named Piety and Faithful and Mary accepted the challenge of the land almost two hundred and fifty years ago, farmers are plowing their fields. They survived the winter, as always, growling and grumbling, also as always, but admitting that the year has four seasons and grateful that a man does not have to make hay in January as well as June and that corn does not have to be planted till May.

We were out in February cutting cedars for posts, though we couldn't get a spade in the ground to repair fences until well into March. You do such chores at the behest of the weather, not of a calendar or the clock. We got out a few sawlogs in January to season till there is slack time between corn planting and haying. Then they will be taken to the sawmill to be cut into boards and planks with which to re-roof the corn crib and the tool shed, probably next fall after the silos are filled, before another winter sets in. One of my neighbors who needed a hernia operation had to put it off twice, once because he had three cows freshening when they had a room at the hospital, the other time because the hospital was full of flu and pneumonia cases. But he finally got fixed up between calves, so to speak.

A man phoned me from down in the city the other day, and after we had settled certain matters about a book of mine he asked what was happening up here in the hills. It was his call, so I told some of these things.

Finally he said, "Nothing really important, then? Nothing earth-shaking?" I said no, I guessed not, just the usual run of things. "The sun still comes up every day," I said. "The earth's still here, and in business." He laughed, then said, "Things are as usual here, too, the same old rat-race. God, I wish I could get away! But somebody has to keep the wheels turning."

I hung up and put on a cap and a windbreaker and boots and went out to help mend fence. But as I walked across the soggy pasture I kept thinking about those wheels he has to keep turning, and finally I paraphrased old Omar Khayyam:

> *"I wonder what those wheels produce*
> *One half so precious as the stuff they grind."*

1964—SUMMER

July, the Year's High Noon

JULY is the year's high, hot noon, even here in the Berkshires where climate is a vendable commodity for those who cater to vacationers. The rest of us, busy with more earthy matters, appreciate the mild mountain mornings, the hot afternoons, and the comfortable nights—good weather for humans and satisfactory growing weather for our crops. But, despite persistent myths, this weather doesn't come for free. We bought and paid for it last December and January. June and July are the annual dividends for those short, icy days and long, sharp-fanged nights we lived with when winter lay heavy on the hills. And even now it isn't exactly loafing weather for most of us.

As soon as the frost was out of the ground we started spring plowing. Then, when the soil had mellowed a bit, we planted the oats and corn, and in off-hours we got down on our knees to the vegetable garden. We bowed our backs and calloused our hands, meeting as best we could the urgencies of the season and the demands of soil and seed. Pastures turned green, oats thrived, corn shivered in May's occasional frosty nights. June brought haying, dawn to dusk. But now, with the first cutting safe in mow and silo, we can catch our breath and enjoy the garden's first yield, fresh peas, crisp salad, early snap beans, creamed new onions, baby carrots. The earth is still good, where it hasn't been salted with poisons. The old tradition of good living on the land is still true.

We did have our troubles with the poison-spray boys again this year. We thought we had that war won, after the President's Science Advisory Commission's report on the toxicity of chlorinated hydrocarbons. But a good many bureaucrats weren't listening either to the report or to the executive order to stop pushing the stuff. And the chemical companies kept right on saying that their poisons were boons, not banes. Some state-sponsored spray programs were curbed, but elsewhere the spray-boys stayed in business-as-usual.

We happen to live on the Connecticut-Massachusetts border, with interstate winds and interstate river in our dooryard. Connecticut curbed the spraying, but Massachusetts didn't. Last spring the Massachusetts Department of Public Resources, presumably devoted to conservation, dusted off its discredited 1963 DDT spray program and urged the town selectmen in the Berkshires to ask for aerial spraying with DDT to control gypsy moths. Last year they said 1963 would be the peak year in the moths' ten-year cycle and warned that unless the woods were sprayed with DDT they would be devastated. Last year the public outcry was so loud that the spray program was canceled, and the woods were not devastated; but the same threat was raised, in the same language, again last spring.

So we had to rally the opposition again, since we cherish our air, our water, our soil, our fish, our birds, our own health, and have confidence in the tenacity of woodlands that have been here for centuries. The battle was on again. And in the midst of it the story broke about all those fish killed by pesticides in the Mississippi. With the heat really on, the Massachusetts Commissioner of Natural Resources made a perfunctory "inspection tour" of the area, said it was all a mistake —the most valid official statement made during the whole controversy—and canceled the spray program. I must add that up to now there has been no wholesale devastation of the woodlands.

So we won the battle with the bureaucrats, again. But I am afraid the war will go on and on. Even as I write this they are still arguing, down in Washington, about the legality, even the propriety, of regulating the multimillion-dollar pesticide industry effectively. As I read the reports of the hearings, when organic poisons are made in million-dollar lots they aren't very poisonous poisons. I'll lay odds, though, that if I brewed aldrin and deildrin and DDT in fifty-dollar lots on my wife's kitchen stove and started peddling them door to door I would have the Feds on my neck before I got two miles from home. But I am not Monsanto or Dow Chemical or American Cyanamid. It seems to make a difference.

The idea that size and numbers automatically create a special kind of integrity and are of themselves virtuous is one of those myths that are too seldom examined for validity. It belongs with blind faith in statistics and belief that anything that costs a billion dollars of public money is worth the price and sacrosanct. The moon-shot program, for example. Or, to get down to earth, the poverty program. Both of them are full of myths, primarily because they are based on statistics and loaded with emotion.

Nobody in his right mind can challenge the necessity of doing everything possible to relieve the plight of the poverty-stricken. Poverty is a cruel and corroding monstrosity in any nation such as ours, both in human and economic terms. But a good deal of both the talk and the statistics thus far have been, to put it mildly, inconclusive.

I keep hearing the term "rural poverty," for example. Yet when I dig into the more intelligible statistics, that term doesn't hold up. Other statistics indicate that roughly one-fifth of the nation is poverty-stricken, using the arbitrary figure of $3,000 a year cash income as the dividing line between privation and bare sufficiency. That would mean around thirty-six million poverty-stricken people. Yet according to the 1962 census figures, the total farm population was only about fourteen million. Even if every farmer in the United States were a pauper there would still be twenty-two million paupers in the cities and towns.

Here in New England we are, I suppose you would say, fortunate in having only 14 per cent of our families in the under-$3,000 group. Connecticut has just under 10 per cent in that group, the lowest rate in the nation.

I recently saw it explained as a consequence of having so few farmers. Only 2 per cent of the population of New England are farm families, compared with 7 per cent for the whole nation. But there again was that "rural poverty" myth—less poverty in New England because there are fewer farm families. Actually, poverty rates even in New England are highest in the urban industrial areas.

Maybe we shouldn't point this out. Maybe we should let the urban-oriented thinkers go right on with their mythmaking and sit here on our farms content with what we have, which is more than those outlanders seem to think. Maybe we should just say that we are lucky and let it go at that. But that doesn't solve anything. And it isn't the whole truth, anyway. Maybe we are lucky, up to a point. But we also planned it this way, this way of life we have and enjoy. We were willing to work for it, and sweat for it, and even to fight for it now and then. As we waged the battle with the bureaucrats last spring to keep our land and water relatively free of poisons.

Perhaps most of all, it doesn't help one bit in the effort toward clarity of thinking and planning. It lets the myths go on and on, pyramiding on each other. When a group of distinguished planners suggested a year or so ago that the way to solve the farm problem was to move several million small farmers off the land and into industrial jobs, we were astonished. It came just at the time when unemployment in industry was beginning to snowball, and when automation was becoming a most troublesome problem. If they had had their way and thrown another two million rural job-hunters into the labor market, God only knows what would be the magnitude of the poverty problem by now.

A few weeks back, while we were in the midst of haying, one of my neighbors stopped past one evening and our casual talk came around to the poverty program. He smiled and said, "I've got the solution."

I asked what he had in mind, and he said, "Move a few million of those poor folks from the cities out to the country. Put them on the land."

"Don't you read the papers?" I asked. "There are too many farmers already!"

"Yeah, I know. In one breath they say there are too many farmers producing too much. In the next breath they say there are all these people in want, can't get enough to eat and wear. It doesn't add up, does it? Too much, and still not enough. Well, my idea doesn't add up either, but it would work. I'd put these people on subsistence farms, ten or twenty acres, where they could earn their keep."

"Make gardeners out of them?"

"Sort of. Give these needy families ten acres apiece, say, and a horse and a cow and a few chickens."

"Where would you get the horses?"

"Never mind that. This is all an impossible idea anyway. But get them started, with a walking plow and a hoe, and a cow for milk and chickens for eggs, and—"

"You know the answer to that, don't you?" I asked.

"Sure. It can't be done. That's the pat answer. It's going back to first principles, so it's impractical. It would give the kids something to do, too, keep them out of juvenile mischief. But the kids don't want to do farm chores. Anyway, it would cost money, ten or twenty thousand dollars a family. How much are we spending on this poverty program, how many million? To do what? Feed and clothe them and train them for jobs in industry that doesn't need them." He shrugged. "You figure it out. I've got to go home and hoe up the garden."

So he went home to hoe his potatoes and pick the horn worms off his big, green tomatoes. And I went out to help pick peas, which we froze that evening for next winter's fare. You can buy peas commercially frozen at the supermarket for next to nothing, as they say, but we like our kind better. And the few pennies we save do help pay the taxes. I don't know what our garden produces, in terms of cash value, but in terms of good eating all winter it is worth the crick in the back in May, the callouses in June, the insect bites and sweat of July and August, and the crick again when we take up the produce to stow away in September.

And I kept thinking about what my neighbor had said, and about the whole mythology of life on the land. Rural America is something of a myth today in almost every aspect, at least to those who live elsewhere and to most of those who deal in big, over-all plans for the population. Land is a potential site for development, or it is open space between cities and their suburbs and other cities and suburbs. People who still live on the land are either big-time farmers or poverty-stricken leftovers who can't get away. Farmland somehow produces excess crops that are an economic problem of gigantic proportions, yet farm life is also underprivileged, chiefly because it isn't urban life. . . . So run the myths.

It doesn't add up. I know I am a traitor for saying so. As a countryman of long standing, and a reasonably content man, I might better keep my mouth shut and let the planners go their way with their ambiguous statistics and unrealistic interpretations. We all live by myths of some kind, and it may be that in the end our whole present era will go down in history as an incredible example of mythological improbability. But now and then, as right now in July, 1964, I am driven to an examination of the more obvious folklore about life as I know it day by day. If I were twenty years younger I might be alarmed by it, but being the age I am and where I am, with my feet on the ground literally at least, I find it amusing in a rather tragic way.

1964—AUTUMN

October and the Color

WHITE FROST came early this year, blackening the squash vines and putting an end to the tomato crop, which was late but bountiful. And the color came early to the woodlands, more vivid than usual by the turn of the equinox. Now it is autumn and we have time to pause and appreciate the beauty and the relative silence. Ear corn is ready to pick, but it can wait a bit. The barns and silos are full, and the pantry and root cellar. It is a good time to be alive and close to the land, a time and place that always help to restore the perspective.

Most of the summer it looked as though perspective was going to be a short crop, as we say. Here in the valley we had one of the best hay years in the memory of white-haired men, but every time we stopped to repair a mower, and often while the mowers were clattering and the balers chomping, we heard angry echoes, some of them as close as Hartford, the staid old capital of this venerable seedbed of abolition. As far as I know, nobody made a pilgrimage to John Brown's birthplace, only twenty-odd miles from here, or to that of Harriet Beecher Stowe in lovely old Litchfield village. But there were pilgrimages and parades elsewhere, and not all of them were happy events.

Then, before we got the last cutting of hay baled and under cover, the echoes from Washington made some of us wonder if fallout and strontium 90 had been reclassified and now were listed with vitamins as beneficial to mankind. I wondered why somebody didn't mention Ben Franklin's comment that there never was a good war or a bad peace. But "war" and "peace" are now relative terms. We have somehow twisted a good many words into strange meanings and given even simple words new and sometimes troublesome connotations.

The other morning I stopped at the hardware store in the village to get a new axe handle, and while I was waiting my turn I said something about "the color." A tall, thin man who moved up here only last spring and still gives the impression of being nervous as a cat looked at me as though I had used a dirty word. "The what?" he asked, with an edge in his voice.

He caught me by surprise, and before I could answer a gray-haired man in a windbreaker spoke up. "The color," he said, "the color in the trees. We've used that word a long time up here, and can't see anything wrong with it now." He is a bred-in-the-bone Connecticut Yankee and lives in the ancestral house famous a hundred years ago as a station on the Underground Railroad. He turned to the clerk behind the counter. "Give me a box of 16-gauge shells, Fred. And new batteries for my big flashlight. Charley and I are going coon hunting tonight." He glanced at the nervous man again. "That's another old word, 'coons.' For raccoons. I hope you don't mind," he added, and he took the shotgun shells and flashlight batteries and walked out, a forthright citizen who refuses to be intimidated by words.

I came home and fitted the new handle to the old axe head, thinking of the time when countrymen carved their own axe handles out of hickory they cut and seasoned from their own woodlots. I haven't the patience or the skill to do that even if I wanted to, which I don't. I have no yearning to go back to the scythe and the flail, the privy and the old oaken bucket. But I do wonder if the old-timers didn't carve and shape a good many sound opinions along with the axe handles and other tools they made. We save time by buying such things ready-made, but time for what? Instead of leisure for thought and careful shaping of opinion, we gear our lives to whirring motors and electronic computers, and we quarrel with ideas when we aren't quarreling with each other.

Then I thought of the harvest and the unaltered progression of the seasons, the way things grow and ripen in the old, old rhythms. Maybe time has changed, along with the times, but only the time we meter out with our swiftly ticking clocks. When I go out of an evening now and see the Big Dipper down on the northern horizon I know that it is pointing the time of all time, just as the clock of the stars has been doing since they were patterned in the night sky. The grass still grows, the oats ripen, the leaves fall, the frosts still come, and winter blows its snowy gales on the same schedule they had before my kind was here to know them. If I abide by that schedule I can manage to live in relative comfort, but the minute I forget it or ignore it, I am courting trouble, and neither clocks nor computers can save me.

Last week we were getting in the winter squash when Albert, our neighbor down the road, stopped to talk. We talked cows and hay and weather, as always. But finally Albert said," I guess I'll walk my lines tomorrow. It gives a man a sense of belonging, sort of."

Walking your lines means going on foot, up through the woods and underbrush, to make sure your property lines are still recognizable. Sometimes you rebuild a pile of stones at a corner, and here and there you mark a tree. Not all the property lines are fenced, especially in the woods and on the steep, rocky hillsides, and they seldom conform to the old stone walls. You have to go to the old deeds, and sometimes you need a compass. But you like to know where they are so that when you take out cedars for fence posts or a few white pine sawlogs for lumber you are sure you aren't trespassing on your neighbor's woodlot.

Anyway, as Albert said, walking your lines gives a man a sense of belonging, and I was glad to hear him put it that way—you belong to the land, not the other way round except in terms of the legalities. And after Albert left I began to wonder if that isn't one big difference between the countryman and his urban cousin. You don't belong to an apartment, even if it belongs to you. It may be home, in a sense, but you really haven't any roots there. I've never known anyone who did, anyway. And I don't see how you can have a sense of security, or even of continuity, without roots somewhere. I even wonder if you can have a sense of identity, in the fundamental meaning, without roots.

Maybe identity isn't important any more, not as important as it once was. The surveys and opinion polls take "samples" and announce that this group thinks so-and-so and that group thinks such-and-such, lumping us by areas or age groups or income or religion, even by race and color. We have become so entranced by numbers and statistics, norms and averages, that the individual is little more than a dot on a chart, a population unit. Maybe this is inevitable, a part of our insistence on reducing everything, even people, to numbers, to accommodate machines that can "think" only in numbers.

This whole process of repudiating the individual apparently inspires some of the younger novelists and playwrights to produce works that express what some critics call "studied confusion" showing "both the futility and vitality of human life." Among the other echoes we heard this past summer were the shouts of angry writers calling each other names almost as vulgar as those heard from the stage and printed in the novels. Largely hidden in the spate of invective were shouts that life was, or wasn't, meaningful and that the individual was, or wasn't, important. Even these dissenters couldn't seem to agree with each other, though they did prove, by their very argument, that there was vitality in their "studied confusion," and that the individual still persists.

I doubt that any of them would agree, but their basic thesis of confusion in the midst of vitality is an old story to the countryman. He lives with it every day of his life, but unlike those who have just discovered it, he also knows that there is fundamental order behind it and that, if he will, he can participate in that order and thus create meaning for himself as an individual. This may give the lie to the charts and the averages, but it is a truth that will persist as long as men live on the land and know the years whole.

The land itself is a kind of confusion of hills and valleys and rivers and ponds; but it is an understandable consequence of great natural causes, not random events. The weather makes its own patterns, only broadly predictable and those predictions short-range; yet it does follow the seasons, and the seasons are as orderly in their sequence as the phases of the moon. True, the seasons as we have chartered them are close to ultimate error and actually violate the solstices and equinoxes more often than they abide by them; we know that winter doesn't wait on the winter solstice, and that the spring equinox isn't going to open apple-blossoms the next day.

Yet the vitality of life is forever asserting itself in the midst of this apparent confusion. Trees grow, grass clothes the valleys, water flows downhill. Woodchucks raid the garden, insects eat the leaves from the trees, foxes eat rabbits, and rabbits eat grass. Yet there is an autumn harvest for man, if he is there to gather it. His trees survive defoliation and seedlings sprout in the woodland litter. Both foxes and rabbits survive and multiply.

And man, if he makes the effort, can find meaning in it, at least to the point of survival, and slow progress in his own affairs. He manages to bring a degree of order out of the confusion, and in that sense achieves meaning for himself. If he is both speculative and inclined to truth he can't avoid seeing that there is fundamental order in the universe and that this world, this environment into which he was born, invites him to participate in order and discover meaning.

It was misty this morning, the valley full of that thin, gauzy autumn mist that comes with a chilly dawn here in the Berkshires. I was up before sunrise and went for a walk before breakfast. I wanted to see the color when the sun first burned its way through, for the trees are shimmery then and the colors most vivid. I walked down the road, and the mist hid the hilltops and hung like a curtain at the edge of the valley. The trees on the hillside were blurred and muted, but those near the road stood out as I had never seen them. A big sugar maple tree was full of golden glory, a tall bird cherry was the color of Burgundy, and a white ash standing in the lower pasture was almost blue, an October shade peculiar to its kind. I wondered why I hadn't noticed them yesterday, or the day before. They were spectacular.

I walked almost a mile, and before I turned back the sun had begun to lift the mist. It hung on the hilltops, but it had been reduced to smoky swirls among the hillside trees. The color, as I had expected, was pristine, clean-washed, and lovely. The hillsides were massed with mingled reds and yellows and tans.

As I came back I kept looking for that maple, that blue ash, and that bird cherry. I knew where they were, exactly, but I had to stop and look to see them. Without the backdrop of mist they were a part of the woodland, a part of the whole huge spread of color on the hillside. I couldn't see the trees for the forest. It was a beautiful forest, a wooded hillside at its autumn prime, but there didn't seem to be an individual tree anywhere.

I came on up the road, which is lined with the mingled purple and white of fall asters, all of the same family yet each with its own color. I passed the big white oak, and the younger black oak nearby, both rooted in the same soil, both bearing acorns. I came to the gnarled old orchard just below the vegetable garden, where windfalls littered the grass beneath the early apple trees and the two late trees still held their dark red fruit. Nature isn't in the teaching business, but a man can learn. It is clear as the nose on a man's face that ripeness and maturity have their own schedule, and that neither force nor intimidation can alter it. Change is inevitable, a part of life; change is planting, and growth, and harvest, in the deliberate progression of the seasons and the years.

I came on home, thinking of countrysides and cities, of population charts and people, of averages and individuals. And of identity, and time, and understanding.

Tomorrow I am going out and walk the lines of my land.

1964–WINTER

Time and Inevitability

SO IT IS almost a new year according to the calendar, and we have safely passed the solstice. That means the daylight is beginning to lengthen, though I have to look in the almanac to prove it, and even then take it on faith. All the change thus far has been in the time of sunset; the sun is still reluctant to rise in the morning and get the fire going. I was up two hours before the sun rose this morning, and if I were of a mind to take credit I might say I was the fellow who routed it out of bed. Being moderately truthful, I have to admit that if I had gone out onto the front porch at 5:15 and whistled and shouted and even commanded, the sun wouldn't have risen then. But when I went out to look at the thermometer—it showed just two above zero—at 7:15, all I had to do was snap my fingers and look off to the east-south-east, and there was the sun peering over the horizon. It was just a matter of timing.

A lot of things are matters of timing. Timing, and inevitability. Take the apples down in our root cellar. We had a big apple crop last fall, the biggest in many years, despite the drought that burned pastures and cut the corn crop in half. We had that big apple crop because of the timing last spring.

We don't grow apples for market. We keep the old trees because we think appleblossoms are something special, and we always have a wonderful wealth of them. But more often than not we have a spell of chill, damp weather just as the apple trees bloom. Apples are fertilized by bees, and bees sulk in chill, damp weather. If the bees stay home sulking, a lot of appleblossoms don't get pollinated, and we have a normal short crop, plenty for our own use but no great excess. Last spring, however, the timing was perfect. The weather was warm and dry right through appleblossom time, and the bees spent sixteen noisy hours a day in the trees. By August the load of fruit was so heavy it literally broke limbs from the trees and, by September, I was stowing apples in the root cellar, ashamed to let them go to waste. That is why there are still a couple of bushels of Baldwins and Jonathans down there. The Snow apples were gone by Thanksgiving; they are our favorites, and they don't keep too well anyway. But the ground under the trees was still red with apples in November, to the delight of deer and raccoons.

That's the way things go. I pleaded for rain at appleblossom time, for the drought was already setting in. The rain didn't come, and the apples did, a result of timing and inevitability. So we made the best of it.

Or take the matter of the bees in Ed's house. That is a bit more complex, but it also was a matter of timing.

Ed lives up the road from me, in a shingled farmhouse that was built when he was a small boy. The summer after it was built was dry. Somehow a grass fire got started in the side yard and reached the house before it was put out. It didn't burn the house but it did scorch the shingles on one end of it. That scorching eventually made the shingles curl a bit, and as the years passed the curling increased. Last winter Ed said he felt the wind coming through that end of the house. He decided to re-shingle it when he got time.

The drought gave him time last summer by easing his field chores, so he bought new shingles and began ripping off the old ones and replacing them. He got as far as the second-floor windows and had to stop. The bees drove him off the staging. There was a swarm of bees in the wall and every time he drove a nail they came boiling out and made it clear that they didn't like the goings-on. Ed wasn't of a mind to dispute them. Besides, he likes honey. If he waited for chilly weather he could dispossess his bees, get a few gallons of honey, and still have time to finish the shingling before winter really set in. So he waited.

Actually, they were my bees. When I came here there was a swarm of bees in a big sugar maple just across the road from my house. They are still there and thriving. From time to time someone suggests that I cut down that tree and get the honey, but even a barrel of honey wouldn't be worth as much as that tree to me. Besides, I like to have the bees there. They are good neighbors, and they pollinate my appleblossoms, among other friendly chores.

Every few years a young queen from the swarm in

my maple tree leads the excess population from the colony to a new home. I watch them swarm, which is a fascinating thing, and fly away in a moiling throng. Usually they head up the mountainside back of the house, where they start a new colony in another hollow tree, but seven years ago they went up the road to Ed's house, found an opening among the shingles on the sunny end, and colonized there. Ed didn't mind. That colony died out the second year. Then, three years ago, another swarm from my tree chose Ed's house and established themselves more successfully. They were the ones that interrupted Ed's shingling.

Ed knows, as most countrymen do, that you pick your time for dislodging a swarm of bees. Particularly if you want to get honey. Anyone can dispose of a swarm in midwinter, but by then they have eaten a good part of the honey. So Ed and Charley, another of my neighbors, chose a dark, chilly day in early November to go after that honey in the walls of Ed's house.

I was there the morning they chose. No problem to it, Charley said. He had handled wild bees a lot of times. He asked Ed what month this swarm arrived and took possession. Ed said it was in May.

Charley nodded and quoted the old saying:

> "*A swarm in May*
> *Worth a load of hay.*
>
> *A swarm in June,*
> *Worth a silver spoon.*
>
> *A swarm in July,*
> *Not worth a fly.*"

"A lot of honey in there," Charley announced, "if they came in May. Short as hay is this year, a load of hay's worth a pile of money."

They set up two ladders and started to remove a sheathing board where the bees had their entrance. Two hammer blows and the bees came streaming out. Both Ed and Charley were up the ladders, but the way they came down they didn't really need any rungs. Ed had two bees under his cap and several more inside his shirt. Charley was slapping so much you couldn't tell where he had them.

We all got safely away and watched the bees go back into the wall. "Wrong time of day," Charley said, and Ed agreed. "Guess we'll have to use smoke," Charley said, and Ed said, "Late this afternoon, when it begins to chill off."

Late afternoon they went at it again. This time the timing was right. They bored holes in the sheathing board, inserted a long tube, built a smudge and blew the smoke in, plenty of smoke. And then they took off the sheathing boards and got at the comb and the honey. There wasn't as much of it as they had expected, twenty-five or thirty pounds, but it was very fine honey, some of the sweetest I ever tasted. Probably basswood honey, since there are lots of basswood trees along the river close by, and the basswood bloomed especially well last June.

Ed finished shingling that end of his house, and we all had honey, which was a consequence of timing. Even to the month that swarm moved in, if I can believe the old saying about a swarm in May. So we came into the winter with things reasonably well in hand, all things considered. Crops were short, but we cut a heavy yield of early hay. Corn didn't do well, but it did fill the silos. Springs failed, but the wells held up; and when Albert, my neighbor down the road, finally gave up on his spring and called in a well driller, he got a flowing well, to everyone's surprise—so much water he had to put in an overflow and channel it into the dry brookbed. One way and another, things compensated even if they didn't even out. The evening-out is a matter of several years, not just a few seasons. That's one thing you learn as a countryman. There may be quick answers and easy solutions to some problems, but the big ones take time.

Like winter. Winter is going to last a good three months, and we know it. Maybe more. Some years it doesn't really take hold till after the solstice, but some years it sets its teeth by Thanksgiving. Some years it spends itself by mid-March, but other years it hangs on into April. Last spring we had a killing frost the first week in June. But over the years it averages out, and we can count on about three months of snow and cold. There are breaks, such as the January thaw, most years. And there are the holidays, every year, which haven't a thing to do with weather but do lighten the heart.

And there is the sun, which within another month will be rising before seven o'clock for the first time since the first week in December. And not setting till after five, with twilight stretching until almost six, especially with snow on the ground. That's what makes February tolerable, the lengthening daylight and the bigger arc the sun cuts across the sky. January, after all, was the Wolf Moon to the Indians, and February was the Hunger Moon. They knew the sun was strengthening, but they also knew it took time for change. They knew the inevitability of wolves and hunger before the relaxation and relief of the New Leaf Moon.

So we do the chores, morning and evenings, by lamplight, and we are grateful for a tight roof, stout walls, and a fire. We wait the winter out, knowing that the ice in the river is not going to be there forever and that the snow in the fields will help to repair the damage of the drought.

We even listen to the old-timer who, though he doesn't believe in astrology, does set store by the zodiac. We are now in Capricorn, he says, the sign of the goat. "Capricorn rules the knees, so watch your rheumatism, and remember to say your prayers," he warns. And he adds, "This is a good time to wean calves, butcher meat, and have teeth pulled. A good time to have your hernia fixed, too." And that is sound enough, probably; a countryman should have repairs made to himself when farm work is slack.

Then the old man says, "After Capricorn, comes Aquarius, the Water Boy. We come into Aquarius on January 20. And after Aquarius comes Pisces, the fishes. Two wet signs."

We want to believe that, too. But when we ask for further advice, he only says, "Keep your feet warm and your head cool, and don't try to hurry things."

So we retreat to the fire again, and are grateful for two epochal events that happened so long ago that only the most ancient myths even try to account for them—the capture of fire and the invention of speech. Without words, to speak or read, and without fire, we would indeed be forlorn in any winter. With them we are armed for most eventualities, though it does sometimes seem that we talk ourselves into a lot of unnecessary troubles. But without words we would still be scrounging among the roots and huddling in caves, so it probably evens out in that area too.

As for fire, there it is on the hearth, and there it is in the sky. And we hold it in its most awesome form in our trembling hands, not yet knowing what to do with it. But as long as we keep talking, with those precious words, we have a chance to find the answer to this problem, too. Maybe it also is a matter of time and inevitabilities. Like my apples. Like Ed's honey. Like winter itself, which always leads to spring.

1965—SPRING

Subtleties and Certainties

IF SPRING arrived with the vernal equinox, full-blown and suddenly visible, half its importance would be lost. The subtleties and the certainties would be lacking; the sense of consequence would not be there. It is far better the way it is, as even Plato knew when he said, "The beginning is the most important part of the work." Spring is not only a beginning, but it has its own beginnings, and every year I am newly aware of my own good fortune in living where I can know them.

On a raw, gusty January day a year ago I went to the village to do an errand at the hardware store and the clerk, a townsman, said he was getting tired of winter. I said that winter was half over and change was in the air. The clerk was skeptical, but before he could argue the point a countryman from down the valley came in and asked for spiles. "Spiles!" the clerk exclaimed. "You won't be tapping maples till March!" And the countryman said, "You spend too much time indoors. You ought to get out and smell the weather instead of just listening to the radio forecasts. I want three dozen galvanized spiles."

The clerk had to go to the storeroom to get them, but the man got his spiles. And I had confirmation of my feeling, my sense of change. Burning pipe tobacco long ago dulled my sense of smell, but even I can detect the difference between an early January snowstorm and one in late February. In early January the snow smells like ice. In late February it has the faint smell of rain. The man who bought the spiles could smell, or perhaps sense in some other arcane way, differences that are beyond me. But I cherish the fact that I can smell the differences in snow, which most people say has no odor at all; it keeps me somewhat in touch with the earth's own truth.

I must add that two days after the little interchange at the hardware store the January thaw set in. It lasted only four days, but, as always, it was a crack in winter's icy door through which we all could get a glimpse of muddy March and burgeoning April. Part of it was the noticeable shift of the sun and the different way the shadows lay. But it was there, the obvious sign of change, and anyone within sight of a pasture or a woodland could see it. Some people saw other things too, such as robins, about which they made quite a fuss. They were resident robins, of course, birds that spend the winter here every year; but the sight of a robin, especially in January, makes people think of spring, even though the thaw ends the next day and winter comes back with a whoop and a dive of the mercury in the thermometer.

This year January passed up the traditional thaw with scarcely a nod. In fact, it was twenty degrees below zero all through late January and the ice on the river, more than a foot thick, didn't even budge. We got our January thaw in mid-February. Snowbanks shrank, brooks came briefly to life, and here came the resident robins to the dooryards. And I noticed that the spiles were out on display at the hardware store. I didn't see my friend from down the valley, though. He was busy about his own affairs. I drove down to see him.

One advantage of living in a place where a grove of maples is called a sugar bush or a sugar orchard is that you know such countrymen. I found him out in the big woodshed he uses as a storage place and workshop. He had just cleaned his sap buckets and he invited me to go up to the sugaring shed with him. We went up the muddy trail into the woods where even the thaw had not cleared out the snow; we had to wind our way among the drifts, and he had to shovel room to open the door. But beside the sugar house was a rick of firewood, several cords of it, that he had cut and stacked there back in November. We went in and he swept out the big, flat pan on its stone fireplace, the evaporator, and scoured it clean. Then, satisfied that all was in order, he led the way out through the woods, roundabout and past a hundred big sugar maples, before we returned to the house.

All the way he kept looking at the trees, watching the birds and the squirrels, the little red squirrels especially, and the chickadees. I didn't have to ask why.

Red squirrels know when the sap is about to begin to run. They have a sweet tooth, and at a proper time they nip off twigs which will create taps at which they can drink the first flowing sap. The chickadees follow the red squirrels, for they too like maple sap and they use the taps the squirrels create. But that day the red squirrels were going about their business and the chickadees fluttered around our heads.

"It'll run early," the sugarman said. "But the early run will be short. End of the month's going to be cold, likely as not."

He was right. Sap did run early. February 22 is the traditional date, in my area. But like all such traditions, it is only approximate. February 22 is only a date on a calendar, after all, and all a tree knows about dates, a sugar maple especially, is summed up in its annual growth rings. A tree measures the seasons and the years, not the days of the month, and sap runs on another schedule. It ran almost a week early this year. But my sugar-man friend had his pails out, spiles set in the south side of thirty or forty trees on a south-facing slope. For a few days we had chilly nights and balmy days, ideal sap weather; then, on Washington's birthday itself, the cold and snow came back, and the sap flow ceased. It didn't run again for almost two weeks.

My friend knew this was going to happen. Don't ask me how he knew. It is enough, for me at least, to know that some men still have such knowledge. I wish I had it. It is one of those subtleties I spoke of, and most of us have to be content with recognizing it when we see it. As I am with the partridges.

The first week in February, which was a cold week by all the canons and in no sense springlike, I was startled when I stepped out the kitchen door on a frosty morning. Three partridges roared out of the big apple tree beside the woodshed. A partridge can be as silent as an owl, or it can scare the wits out of you. These didn't scare me, but they certainly startled me. Then I almost said, "Thank you" as I watched them rocket toward the woods. They had been down eating apple buds, and they had told me that spring was on its way.

Partridges eat buds all through the winter, mostly the tiny buds of birch and aspen. My friend, Morris, who has hunted partridges all his life and has forgotten more about them than I shall ever know, tells me he has found such fare in their crops in mid-November, before the deep cold set in. But they don't come down to the dooryard for apple buds until something beyond my human understanding begins to happen. I suspect, though I really do not know, that two things happen. First, at that precise point the buds are enriched with a vital element, perhaps a vitamin, that was not in them until that particular moment. And, second, the partridges need that vitamin, or whatever is newly present in the buds, and sense the time when it will be there. I do know that if I cut apple twigs to force in the house before the partridges come down, I get no blossoms; if I cut them after the partridges come, I do get blossoms.

But even more important is what happens down at the root of things; at the roots of the apple trees, for instance, under a foot of snow and several feet of soil.

Some combination of daylight length, sun's angle, and perhaps even more mysterious matters, penetrates the snow and the soil and informs the roots. Something vital begins to happen. The buds, high above the roots and open to the icy wind, begin to quicken. I will not say they know that spring is coming, but they do begin to prepare for it. The whole urgency of the apple tree begins to assert itself. And the partridges know it, even though I don't until the partridges tell me.

I must add this note. Two days after the partridges were in the apple tree, Morris telephoned me. He had been housebound with a cold and the miseries in general, but had recovered enough to go outdoors and "smell the weather," as he said. And he asked, "Have the partridges been down to your apple trees yet?" I told him they had. "It figures," he said. "I had a feeling they'd be down for buds about now." Morris didn't even have to see those partridges; he knew, he sensed it.

After February's last-week spasm of snow and cold I was impatient with a housebound life. I had to go out and look for the March that should be at hand. I went up the mountainside, expected to find little more than the tag ends of winter, the untidy litter out of which spring always builds its green beauty. I found those tag ends, of course; but in a tiny pocket on the mountainside, where a seep spring long ago created a pocket-size bog that would fit into our kitchen, I found something else.

A few alder bushes grow in the damp soil there, and when I stopped to look at them I saw a honey bee. No bee should have been out that day. Then I saw the reason. Half a dozen catkins on one of the alders were partly open. Alder catkins appear in the fall and hang on the twigs all winter, tight as a fist. They don't mature their pollen and relax their scales to release it until early spring, when the tiny female blossoms open. There wasn't a female blossom in sight, but a few of the male catkins had relaxed enough to free a few grains of pollen. Eager males, they were already spilling their sperm, just in case there was a ready ovule. And that bee, perhaps from the wild swarm in one of my sugar maples a quarter of a mile away, had come and found it.

So there on the mountainside, on a raw first day of March, a few alder catkins and a hungry bee gave me a glimpse of April and even of May, when my dooryard will be sweet with pollen and loud with bees. I didn't see spring, but I did see another of the beginnings of spring. I saw subtleties and certainties and I was aware of consequences to come.

Coming down the mountainside I knew that spring was already marching north, somewhere down beyond the horizon, down where the thirty-two-degree isotherm was lapping at the hills of Georgia and lower Carolina, and for a few minutes I wished I were down there to come back with it. I thought how spring moves north, at a pace which a man on foot can follow even if he is a leisurely walker who likes to stop and look at the trees and listen to the birds. It travels only about sixteen miles a day, and when it comes to a hill it slows down even that leisurely pace, climbing only a hundred feet or so a day. I remembered how in April, I can look across the valley at Canaan Mountain, six miles away, and watch spring climb its rugged slopes; literally see the slow daily upward climb of green among the trees.

Then I thought that by April the commitment is complete. Chives in the garden will have new shoots, rhubarb will be thrusting up red, crinkly leaves, crocuses will have bloomed and faded, daffodils will be in fat bud. Spring plowing will be under way and every breeze will be rich with the fecund odor of spring. And I was content to be here, sensing the subtleties of spring, no matter how dulled my senses are. Here, sensing spring's beginnings. Like so many other things, it is spring's first beginnings that are most exciting. Full-blown spring is a kind of conquest completed. It has always been the young pioneer who makes the most fascinating history, for he is shaping the future. First beginnings are the time when dreams are born, the visioned shape of great achievement still to come. But first must come the certainty, the belief, the subtle sensing of change and the inevitability of tomorrow.

So I came back down the mountainside content to live with March and await April. Content to be rooted here, not walking north with spring; to let spring come to me, as it always comes, in the whirr of partridge wings, in the rise of sap in the maple trees, in the first spill of pollen from an alder catkin. I was not only content but specially privileged to know the subtleties as well as the certainties and once more to be a part of the eternally miraculous beginning of spring upon the land.

1965–SUMMER

The Green Achievement

BY JULY it is so summery that it is easy to forget spring. We are surrounded by so much evidence of achievement that what went into it, like the details of so many beginnings, is a part of some dim yesterday. It seems impossible that today's bee hum and insect buzz, reaching corn, ripening oats, and new hay in the barn were egg and seed and wakening root only a few weeks ago. July seems so complete that it might have been here for years and so enduring that it could continue for another decade.

Summer brings this dual sense of time, particularly in the country. There is the foreverness, this almost droning completion; and there is the day to day urgency and the sense of time passing swiftly. Days are long and full. To the countryman they are a kind of delayed payment for the short days of abbreviated demand that were his in January. Now he buys his winter leisure. Yet he lives in the midst of a world that has done its hurrying, passed its springtime urgency, a world where grass grows silently, and high cumulus clouds drift lazily across the sky; where fireflies sparkle the night, luna moths fray their fragile wings at screened windows, and whippoorwills call monotonously.

Spring is pressure building up to the green explosion of May, and May itself is such energetic haste that it seems impossible that its major sounds are birdsongs. The urgencies carry over into June before they begin to ease toward the fulfillment of July. By now we are almost as sated as the noontime bumblebee, accepting this green world as the norm, forgetting April.

We had a late, cold spring up here in the hills. This was the year to plow and re-seed the home pasture, and Albert was frosted out twice before he got the old sod turned and harrowed to his liking. There was so much frost in the ground the third week in April that it was like plowing shale, and Albert, bundled in winter clothing when he should have been in shirt sleeves, said, "It's ridiculous, plowing in weather like this. But we can't wait any longer." He felt the pressures, even as the trees and the grass. There was work to be done before May and June. So he plowed and harrowed and seeded, and now the new grass is almost knee-high. Looking at it the other day, Albert said, "You kind of forget, in March and April, how the season always evens out."

Maybe we need a late, cold spring now and then to keep our perspective healthy. There is the temptation to look in the almanac instead of watching the ground underfoot, to turn to statistics instead of seeing the obvious facts. Spring seldom begins on the vernal equinox, and I have yet to see a summer that waited for the solstice. The almanac, though mathematically accurate right down to the second, is only approximate in the practical terms of the earth itself. It might be simpler if you could say with certainty that the equinox would mark the absolute end of freezing weather. But life isn't that simple, as we are reminded year after year. The best we can do is split the year into quarters and make our compromises with the seasons as they come. When man lived close to the land he knew, every day of his life, that you have to lean with the wind and dress for the weather. He was aware of the stars and their moving patterns, but his feet were on the ground. He knew that a compromise was, at the root, a mutual promise—nature would do her part and, if he would survive and prosper, he must do his; that was all there was to it.

Of all the seasons, summer probably is the least demanding. The major work of the year, the sprouting and the leafing, is done. The vast canopy of chlorophyll is spread and transforming sunlight and air into basic foodstuffs without a murmur. The grass grows in every pasture and hayfield, even at the roadsides, fundamental nourishment for all red-blooded life, and no one is compelled to acknowledge the intricate food-chain that leads from a grass root to his own sentient flesh. The fertile blossoms drop their petals and fatten the seeds in their ovules. Berries ripen, pods mature, roots and tubers and bulbs stow their stores of nourishment. The earth prepares its own bounty.

Even the farmer has his options now, though his choices are dictated by his own needs and ambitions.

He can make hay or let the grass go to seed. He can tend his fields or let the weeds take over. He can lie in the shade or go fishing or do the work that should be done. Happily for those who would starve without his crops, he knows even in July that though the living is easy now he will go hungry next winter if he plays proverbial grasshopper instead of emulating the ant and the bee. He has the choice, so he works, takes care of his crop, insures its yield.

A summer vacationer stopped past the other day and said, "If I could find a farm like this, which just runs itself, I'd be tempted to buy." I had to tell him to resist the temptation if that was the way he felt. No farm runs itself, even though it may seem to in midsummer. We have reduced the running to what is probably a minimum, by leasing the pastureland to the dairyman just down the road and letting the woods grow pretty much as they would if we weren't here. We take care of the dooryard, tend a big vegetable garden, encourage quite a lot of flowers, and do our best to keep the brush and weeds at bay. But the land doesn't "just run itself." If we left it to itself, the pastures would be overrun by birch and sumac, the fences would rot and rust, and we would soon be living in a tumble-down house crowded by a thicket.

Man is essentially a transient tenant on the land. Nature tolerates him, I suppose one could say, simply because he invented the axe and the plow. Nature's function is growth and proliferation, and unless a man is ready to maintain his foothold he will lose his acres. So we cut grass and chop brush and repair the fences and try to keep erosion from gullying the pastures, work that doesn't show, except in its neat results, in July. As I said earlier, we plowed and re-seeded the home pasture last spring, not because there wasn't grass in it but because the grass had thinned out and weeds were taking over. Now it is a beautiful green pasture, and my vacationing visitor thought it would be an ideal place to lay out a nine-hole golf course. Maybe it would, if one wanted a nine-hole golf course. We happen to prefer a pasture, with Albert's cows, which actually isn't half as much work to maintain. But if I had said that to Albert last April, when he was plowing the frosty soil to keep ahead of May, he would have thought I was out of my mind.

Summer is deceptive that way. It makes you think of Eden and forget what happened after Adam ate the fruit. Maybe it is Eden, after all; and maybe we, too, lose our summer-Eden only when we eat the ripened fruit of September. If so, it is a good arrangement, having our Eden every year, forfeiting it, then working our way back into grace through winter and spring. It could be that the very name of fall has a dual meaning. But that's something to ponder in October, not just now.

Now we live in the midst of green achievement, April brought to July's fulfillment. Even a July thunderstorm has a majesty quite unlike the warm, all-day rains of spring, a special atmospheric achievement. We had such a storm only a few days ago, and I am sure we shall have others before the month is out.

It was one of those hot, still days when even such a

minor chore as hand-weeding the lima beans brings out the sweat. There wasn't a cloud in sight all morning, but the sky was that steely blue that seems to intensify the sun. I weeded, and sweated, and stopped from time to time to admire the sweet corn, tall and green and sturdy. But by noon there was a vague tension in the air that made the birds restless. They called to their fledglings with more than the usual apprehension.

About one o'clock a low thundercloud appeared in the northeast. The sky seemed to darken, though the sun still shone clear and brassy. The air was breathless, leaves hanging listless on the trees. When a crow cawed the sound echoed as in a vast, closed room.

The cloud rose swiftly. It became a darkening bank that covered half the sky. There was a swish, far off, as of sudden wind in the trees on a far hill. Lightning flashed across the cloud bank, turning it black and ominous for a quick instant. Half a minute later the thunder rolled down the valley. A pause, another flash, closer, and the thunder bounded from hill to hill, echoing, seeming to shake Tom's Mountain. Still another flash, and a crashing roar of thunder shook the house and made us wince.

A gust of wind swept down the river and the dancing water was like a hurrying wave. The trees shook. Not a bird made a sound. Then deep, tense silence again, until another flash was followed in no time at all by the crash of thunder, a strike too close for comfort.

The darkness on the woods far up the mountain turned to gray, and the gray marched down the slopes. We could hear the rush of rain, the pelt and swish and muted roar. But still there was not a breath of wind down here, the air tautly calm after that one breathy gust down the river. On the mountainside we could see the trees swaying and we could hear the rush of wind coming.

Then the rain came down the river, a gray, steely curtain. The whole valley seemed to shiver. The trees trembled. Their leaves rustled and pattered. Then the rain struck the house, in a rush, and the whole river was leaping in little spurts to meet the rain. The maples swished and roared and their gray trunks turned black as the rain streamed down them. The apple trees shook and spattered small green apples on the grass, wet and shiny.

And as swiftly as the rain came, the darkness passed. It was a silvery world, the air laced with silvery threads, almost glowing as the rain sheeted down. A few more flashes of lightning, a few more thumping, echoing peals of thunder that rattled the windows, and the violence of the storm had passed. But the rain continued another twenty minutes, such a downpour as we get only in one of July's more spectacular thunderstorms.

When it was all over, the sun shining in a clean, clear sky and the air cool and refreshing, the trees still dripping and the roadsides like young brooks, I put on my mud-boots and went out to straighten up the sweet corn in the garden.

That's the way it is in July. You go out in the morning to tend your crops, and you feel like the master of the land, if not of all creation. You know you made your deal, your compromise, promising to give it your sweat in return for the soil's fertility. You admire the sweet corn, silked out and already fattening ears. It is an achievement, something you, like April, gave its start and now see coming to July's fulfillment. You can almost taste its sweetness. Then a thunderstorm comes, clapping your ears with thunder, soaking you to the skin, and flattening your carefully tended corn. So now you have to get down on your knees in the mud, straighten it up, give its roots new and firmer footing. You have to make obeisance to the soil with which you made that compact. You have to admit that you are only a man, after all, not a god.

Then you remember spring, and beginnings. You remember that only a few weeks ago there was frost in that soil, that you had to stir it and plant it; you remember how those seeds sprouted and grew; you remember May, and the incredible green explosion. You remember that summer is a consequence of spring, not a season remote in time, here forever. You are aware of time's other dimension.

Summer provides its own correctives. If it were all bee-drone and clover-sweetness we might forget that there is a wholeness to the year, every year. We might forget that honey is concentrated labor as well as pollen and nectar free for the bees' taking.

Summer on the land is spring completed and fall in the making, time in both its strange dimensions.

The Hoarding Days

WE CALL OCTOBER the Hoarding Days, forgetting for a while the economic theories of planned deficits. Maybe "hoarding" isn't the best word to use, though it simply means stowing away, laying up for future need. But we think of a miser and his hoard rather than of a farmer and his reserves, which are as natural as the seasons. It could be that "thrift" is a better term.

Here in the Connecticut Berkshires we did have a deficit this past summer, though, an unplanned deficit of rain. We had a drought that began in May and didn't relax all summer. Except in fortunate local areas, we had a short hay crop, pastures played out by the end of July, springs dried up, wells failed, brooks shrank to trickles, and rivers sank to their lowest levels in years. The corn crop was spotty. So we started early to gather in whatever was available in the way of forage, knowing that winter lay ahead. Whether we were hoarding or just being thrifty, we followed the old practice of doing the best we could with what was at hand. If we can make out till next spring, maybe next year things will be better. A farmer thinks in such terms, year to year rather than day to day. He knows that nothing grows overnight except mushrooms.

So we hoarded, from garden and field and woodland, and we are still stowing things away. I dug the potatoes a few days ago, not a very good crop but enough to justify the digging, and we have put away all the apples we will need, canned the pears and frozen the beans. The late garden didn't amount to much, but a man can eat only so much pumpkin and Hubbard squash, after all, and we did get the early sweet corn. I suppose the coons needed the late corn more than we did, thought I do think they might have found just as good fare in the woods if they had put their minds to it.

And now when I look around I can't for the life of me feel guilty about this hoarding because thrift is as natural a process as growth. The big sugar maples in front of my house are as thrifty as I am, maybe even more so. Right now they are magnificent in shimmering golden leaf, breath-taking when the early morning light strikes them. The whole woodland, in fact, is practically at its peak of color, soft maples crimson, birches bronzed, white ash almost blue. And at first thought all this display of color is sheer extravagance. Technically speaking, the color is a matter of sugars and acids left over in the leaves when the trees stopped replenishing their chlorophyll. Within another week or so those leaves will be discarded, thrown to the wind.

But those leaves, for all their color and chemical content, are not waste at all. True, the trees shed them.

The trees have withdrawn sap and other vital substances into limb and trunk and root—a hoarding process, by the way. But when the leaves fall, they will go back to the earth and become mulch and leaf mold to protect and nourish future growth. The trees don't rake and burn those leaves. They shed them and they, or other plants, will use them in one form or another in the future. Rob any woodland of its mulch and leaf mold for a few years and the trees begin to starve and die. The whole process of plant life is one of thrift. Man may call it an untidy mess, but nature thrives on the litter that accompanies every autumn. Nature is a hoarder.

The animals and insects, of course, are classic hoarders—the squirrels, the chipmunks, the field mice and all their kin, and the ants and the bees. Squirrels are busy right now in the oaks and hickories. I never go into the woods without seeing their hyperthyroid industry and hearing their warning chatter—"What are you doing here, trying to steal our harvest of nuts and acorns?" Stiff-tailed chipmunks are busy every sunny day, filling their winter granaries and gathering fluff for their winter nests. Bees are working overtime, gathering the last supply of pollen and nectar from late goldenrod and asters. On warm, sunny afternoons the ants are gleaning tiny seeds and stocking their tunnel storage bins.

Less provident insects, those whose short lives create no such winter need, do their hoarding in another way. They hoard life itself, in egg and pupa, to pass on to another generation. Even the woolly bear caterpillars, hurrying now to find shelter, hoard their precious spark of life in hibernation; next spring they will undergo the next stage of their astonishing life and become pink-tinged yellow moths that feed hungrily on the plantain I try to eliminate from my lawn. I may wish such insects as gypsy moths and tent caterpillars were less successful at hoarding life in the egg; but they, if they were anything more than concentrated reflexes and hungers, might wish that I and all my kind were less proprietary of the trees they feed upon to sustain that life.

In every way I can imagine, I should be grateful for nature's thrift. Without it, we would all be in trouble, and it doesn't matter how clever and ingenious we may be in devising substitutes for the things that grow. Even in the matter of moisture—I am sorry, but the drought has made rain a matter of major consequence—even in terms of moisture, nature is unfailingly thrifty. The water cycle is one of the certainties of our atmosphere: water is evaporated from the oceans, the lakes and the rivers, becomes clouds, and falls back to the earth as rain or snow, only to flow or seep back to the great reservoirs, where the cycle is forever repeated. Those who calculate such matters say that the earth has as much water today as it had ten million years ago. If one area suffers drought, as ours did this past summer, it is a consequence of shifting winds or some other atmospheric variant. If we got too little, some place else got too much. The total remains the same.

So we wait for the fall rains, hoping the year's deficit will not all be made up in one storm. Hoping, in other words, for a degree of moderation, but not really counting on it. Knowing, when we stop to think, that what we call norms are nothing more than averages.

Meanwhile, the flickers and the robins and the red-winged blackbirds have gone south for the winter. The blue jays and the crows pretty well possess the countryside, though the chickadees and the tree sparrows and the little woodpeckers now come regularly to the dooryard for handouts. None of them is a hoarder, though I was surprised last summer to find that the chickadees do have a degree of thrift. A neighbor of mine, who has a particular fondness for the chickadees, fed them sunflower seeds even in August. He noted that they shelled the seeds and carried the kernels away instead of eating them, and when he patiently traced their course he found that they hid those sunflower kernels in a clump of red cedars, tucking each kernel tightly into a crevice in the bark or into a tuft of scaly foliage at a twig tip. We looked among the trees and found dozens of those hidden seeds. So even those little beggars are not mere mendicants at the window sill.

The migrants left, and other migrants arrived. In a few more weeks the chilly wind will be alive with juncos and snow buntings, come down from the north to winter here. I heard a flock of geese go over night before last, gabbling like a pack of small dogs yapping. By the time of the full moon, on October 20, the goose flights probably will be almost daily. That will be the Hunter's Moon, and coon dogs will be belling the night, the few remaining coon hunters following them, and sitting on the hillsides and telling stories that have almost become legend now.

An old friend of mine who retired from farming a couple of years ago after forty-odd years of tending cows and growing corn and hay stopped past the other afternoon, looked up the glowing mountainside, and said, "Come full moon, I'd like to go on just one more coon hunt. If I had a coon dog like the one I used to have." And he stayed for an hour, telling stories about dogs and coon hunts. I'd heard them all, one time and another, but listening to him, I knew what a precious thing is this thrift by which we can relive the past without really going back.

Finally Charley said, "How about it? If I can get hold of Sam Sawyer, we could have one more coon hunt. Sam had a coon dog, last I heard. We could go up on Cooper Hill and start from there, in that big corn field, and work right down here to your woods."

I said, "Fine," and Charley left, content.

Maybe we will go, maybe we won't. It doesn't matter much either way, because there is that whole store of coon hunts of the past into which we can dip at any time, thanks to the way we hoard our remembered pleasures.

Especially in autumn, which is a kind of memory forever renewed. Maybe we treasure our autumns here in this hilly corner of New England because it is the year's memorable season. Spring is a sometime thing, up here, with March sometimes lapping over into May, and May often taking a week right out of July. Summer is a busy season for the countryman, not the vacation time that the outland visitors seem to think it is; and summer can be hot and sweaty when you are up to your armpits in the hay harvest. Winter is often rugged, with a full measure of snow and ice. But autumn is wonderful.

Autumn sometimes begins here in late August, and even when summer persists there is the glow of goldenrod, the flame of impatient sumac, the purple of Joe Pye weed, blue vervain and New England asters. By September the summer pressures begin to relax, outdoors as well as in. The garden's tomato crop has passed its peak. Ensilage corn is already in the silo and hay is in the mow. Field corn can stand on its rustling stalks till the farmer gets to it with his picker. First frost puts an end to gardening, thank goodness, and a man can take his time about the neatening up for the winter. By October, autumn has settled in. With luck and normal weather—which is to say, the weather that comes four years out of five—autumn will continue all the way to Thanksgiving. In specially favored years, it will continue till Christmas week.

Now that I have said this, I see that autumn isn't really so long, after all, only three months at most, and a part of that is very frosty, the kind of weather that would be called winter in a good many places. What I am thinking, I suppose, is that our autumns, here on the land, are a kind of leisurely summary of the year. The trees have summarized their annual growth, the pastures and hay fields are summarized in our barns, the gardens are consolidated in our root cellars and pantries, and even the days and nights somehow achieve a kind of recapitulation. Indian Summer days come, without the heat and humidity; and Squaw Winter comes without burying us under snow. Man is invited to participate in all this, and if he lives on the land he can't very well do anything but participate. Autumn is all around him, everywhere he looks or walks, urging him to slow down to the season's own pace and accept the world on its own terms, not his, for a change.

Those terms are not really difficult to accept. Autumn, after all, is only another phase in the endless cycle of growth and time. We happen to find beauty in it, and if we are fortunate we see serenity in it. There is an incorruptibility, in a sense, that not even man can distort, for autumn is both a consequence and a prolonged occasion beyond human management. It is a kind of perfection, an achievement and fulfillment, of a degree so rare in the affairs of man that if we stop and consider it we cannot help being awed. It isn't completion, even though it is ripeness and maturity. Completion is a human concept. Nature is change and a constant going on; and autumn is an inevitable part of that change.

I saw the sun rise this morning just a trace south of true east. Today's daylight will be three minutes shorter than was yesterday's. The rising sun in the maples made a dazzling glow, and at noon the light beneath those trees was more golden than the sunlight itself. Yet within another week or ten days those yellow leaves will fall and rustle along the road in the breeze, and I can stand beneath those trees and see the gleam of the stars forming the great square of Pegasus almost overhead. The red fox barks and the barred owl hoots in the half-moon's light, and the insect chorus is silent. My season's hoarding is almost finished, and I can face the winter with confidence in my reserves. That, to me, is October. But it is not new. It is so old that it is a part of time's own hoard, and I am awed only because it always seems so new to me when it comes, such a new, magnificent achievement.

1965—WINTER

Wholeness and Holiness

As FAR BACK as the race memories run, the winter solstice has been a time of questioning and wonder that led to rediscovery of the basic certainties. It wasn't by chance that it became the occasion for religious events that we now speak of, in our offhand way, as The Holidays. It was, and still is, a holy time in the deepest sense. When we see the sun stand still, far off toward the south, and then swing north, lengthening the daylight after steady weeks of abbreviation, we are witness to a cosmic miracle.

It doesn't really matter that we now explain it in terms of celestial order and rhythm, with their inevitable consequences. Rationalize it as we may, there is some force behind it; and all our intricate calculations can do is state the How and the Why in terms of elaborate equations. They can't get at the What, which lies beyond, the inevitability itself. We have to take that on faith.

A wise old countryman once said to me, "Every winter I have to renew my belief." And when I asked, "Belief in what?" he said, "My belief in believing."

That is the gist of it, stated with the utmost economy. Belief is easy in June, with summer all around you. In fact, doubt is difficult in a green and hospitable world. The test comes in December, when you have to believe that onsetting winter will pass. You have to muster the deep-down belief that hope is not foolish and faith is not futile. You have to believe in your own believing.

There is, of course, a fundamental faith rooted in the land. It is as simple as a seed, as inevitable as the seasons. In spring, the farmer who plants a field partakes of that belief. If he were given to doubt he would hoard the seed, breadstuff in itself, wondering whether it would sprout or rot in the ground. But, believing, he plants and watches the expected sprouting. He tills and tends, and when the time comes he takes his harvest.

There is another solstice in June, and perhaps if we had time in June we would take more note of it. But in June we are busy making hay, stowing the fragrant bales for the future. In haying time we are thinking of the plenty, the faith and fecundity inherent in the seed. The days and weeks of want and hunger may be somewhere in the back of our minds, but far back; the inevitability for which we are preparing is still remote. Summer is still upon us.

By September we have wearied of summer. Our barns and silos are full, our pantries and our cellars are provisioned. We have had enough of sweat and muscle strain and want to sit and enjoy the fruits of our faith and leisure. We welcome the autumn equinox and hard frost, an end to the growing season. We are ready for Thanksgiving.

Despite the pious stories about its origins, I sometimes wonder if there weren't among those first celebrants of Thanksgiving at least a few who were secretly as grateful for an end to labor in the fields as for the harvest itself. True, they hadn't yet faced the winter's test of faith, but they certainly had seen other winters come and go. I know that up here in the hills where memories are long and traditions treasured we tend to make short shrift of the thanks and congratulate ourselves on our own industry and foresight. We sacrifice the turkey, glorify the potato, the onion, and the turnip, outdo the forgotten inventors of pemmican with our mincemeat pies. We do appreciate the plenty, but we also take credit for hard work well done. This may indicate a lack of proper piety, but it is not exactly an innovation. Man has always appreciated a good meal and a chance to rest, and his prayers have most often been for mercy rather than to offer thanks. It takes the shadow of imminent disaster to get most of us down on our knees.

But by mid-December we are aware of such a shadow. The year approaches the climax of the eternal drama, the struggle between light and darkness. Fundamentally, there are only two great dramas, the conflict of life and death, and that of light and darkness. Ever since he has been capable of wonder, man has been aware of them, and inevitably he has incorporated the parallels into his religious rites and beliefs. Knowing the Why and the How, even without the elaborate equations, he long ago reached for the What and sought to ally himself with it. The ancient pagans measured shadows, built bonfires at the critical time, cut green boughs and begged the gods of What to keep their universe in order. We measure orbits and leave it to the astral physicists to keep things going properly. We talk of inevitability, at least for a few more million years; but we take that inevitability on faith. Like the old countryman, we believe in our own believing.

A few weeks ago, in the first real snowstorm of the season, I saw Albert walking about our lower pasture. I say "our" because our land adjoins and Albert rents my pastureland. I was about to go out for an afternoon breath of air, so I put on a heavy coat and cut across the pastures to join him.

He saw me coming and waited. As we walked along the fencerow he said, "I was wondering if we ought to plow this lot next spring and re-seed." I knew that was an excuse, not a reason. I also knew he would come to the reason in his own time.

We walked about the pasture, making a show of examining the grass already grizzled with snow. We stopped to watch a flock of juncos, like gray snowflakes caught in a gust, as they flew out of a weedy corner. Albert is the kind who will stop his tractor and turn off the motor to listen to a bluebird in April. We almost stepped on a cottontail before it leaped from a grass clump and darted to safety in the brush. And as we approached a barberry tangle two ruffed grouse took off with a roar, startling us as always, and rocketed into the woods beyond. Albert watched them, a slight smile on his face, and said, "We ought to grub out that barberry," then added, still smiling, "if it was ours. But it's theirs," and he nodded toward the vanished partridges. "They planted it, and their crops are always full of the berries, this time of year."

We went on. The snow had become so thick a curtain that I could scarcely see my house, only a quarter of a mile away. We cut back toward the road, and Albert, who has lived on this land all his life, said, "The way this snow's coming, it'll stay on the ground for a while. I don't mind winter, but I have to get out and feel the ground under my feet before it pens me in."

We came to the barway, went through and put the bars back up. Albert went down the road, toward his house, his barns, and his cows. He had given me his reason, and I came on home.

In a way, he was saying pretty much the same thing a woman said at a small gathering the other evening. She and her husband came up here from the city last spring and bought a small house and a few rural acres for week ends and vacations. They returned to the city at the end of the summer, but they came back and settled in for good just before Thanksgiving.

I asked if the Big Blackout, the incredible power failure that paralyzed the Northeast early in November, had been responsible. The city, I said, must have been a rather frightening place that night. We were lucky up here, being in a rare pocket with a local power source. We were blacked out less than one minute. Did they come back thinking our luck would hold in another emergency?

She laughed. "No. We made our decision a week before it happened. We really made up our minds last summer, though we didn't tell each other for several weeks. We talked all around the subject before we really faced it. Then we took stock. Last summer John was offered a part-time job in the village, and with that we could manage comfortably. So it became a matter of intangibles, what we really wanted, and what the city offered—theatres, concerts, art exhibits. And *Things.* We weighed them all and decided we had to take life directly, not someone else's interpretation of it. So here we are, ready to face winter and welcome spring. I went out the day before Christmas to walk in the woods and I discovered snowflakes. Imagine! I never *really* saw a snowflake before."

She went on to talk about the magic of hoar frost and the beauty of snowflakes, about the color of the hills at dawn and dusk, the wonder of sunset and moonrise and stars. And I knew it wasn't just the country, or sun, moon, stars, and glittering frost and snow—it was all of them, and more. It was discovering the wonder and the mystery of life, taken directly, before someone else's interpretation penned them in beyond escape.

We come now, of course, to what the Indians called the Wolf Moon. We have dulled the fang of winter, even here in the country, but we still know the reasons for that naming. But—and here is the core of meaning in the holidays we are observing—we can face even the Wolf Moon with confidence, knowing it, too, will pass. We have renewed our belief.

Each year, at the time of the solstice, we go up into

the woods on our mountainside to choose a tree and gather greens for Christmas. And each year we pause at the edge of the woods and I examine a small clump of gray birches at the edge of the brook. I look for buds and catkins. The buds are very small and they lie snug to the twigs. I once opened such a bud and found in it a furled leaf so small I needed a ten-power glass to trace its outlines, but unmistakably a leaf. The catkins are like miniature inchworms dangling here and there from twigs, male catkins tightly closed but with a store of pollen fine as motes.

This year I looked, as always, and those birches, though winter dormant, had leaf and blossom ready and waiting for April, made ready before first frost put an end to last summer. I knew that something in the living entity that is a tree had prepared for the going-on, for the time beyond the winter solstice.

There, beside the iced-in brook on the late December mountainside, was the promise that the winter solstice would pass and the sun would resume its certain course toward another vernal equinox. But, being of ancient lineage ourselves and with the questioning and the wonder in our hearts, we went on and chose the tree and cut the boughs. We brought them home, being racially committed to the green offering and the symbolic lights. Beyond the bud and the catkin, we had to express our own believing.

And when Christmas came we observed the rites, doubly aware of the holiness; for the rites are both an acknowledgment of the mysterious What, which the equations cannot reach, and the links with the long,

long line of our own kind. And with the What itself. For all its teeming populations, this world is essentially a lonely place without those links. Rationality is not enough. It does not have all the answers. We need a few enduring mysteries, and no doubt we shall always have them. We need acceptance of such a simple mystery as how a birch tree knows there will be another spring and prepares for it. And if I am being anthropomorphic in saying that the tree knows, so be it. Is our kind of knowledge the only kind we can accept, in the face of evidence all around us?

So we observed the rites. And I also observed the shadows. Specifically, the shadow cast on the living-room wall as the sun shines through the window facing east. I saw a slight shift from the place that shadow touched the wall only a few days before. The shift was only the breadth of my little finger, but it meant that the sun had moved, as we say, back toward the north by one finger's breadth. Another week and the change will be two fingers' breadth. That I know as surely as I know that the sun will rise. The solstice safely passed, we observed symbolic Christmas. Our faith is replenished.

Now we can go on, facing this Wolf Moon, remembering that as the days lengthen the cold will strengthen, that February will be heaped with snow, that March will be both February and April, and that after the vernal equinox we will wait impatiently for spring on earth. Winter has begun to pen us in, but eventually we will walk the pastures again, the quickening soil beneath our feet, root and seed alive and reaching for rain and sunlight. This we know. We have no option, no choice except belief.

It is late afternoon and the bitter year-end wind is dying down. The sky that darkened in early afternoon seemed to lighten a little while ago. It has begun to snow. At first the snow came in huge clots, clumped flakes that splattered as they struck the window pane. Now they have begun to separate, falling like feathers. The sky has disappeared. I put on a dark coat and go out to be a part of the evening, and when I look up I am in the midst of an incredible galaxy of snowflakes. I return to the porch, and under the porch light I see the individual flakes on my coat sleeve. I cannot understand the infinite variety of the snowflakes, but there they are, crystalline perfection so fragile that my slightest breath reduces them to drops of moisture.

I return to the dooryard and stand there in the falling snow. The dusk deepens. Night is at hand. Soon I shall come back inside, to the security of walls and roof and fire, fruit of my own providence. But for a little while I am one with the dusk and the snow, and I am full of wonder. Here is wholeness and holiness, and I partake, knowing that beyond the reasons lies belief.

1966—SPRING

April and the National Conscience

THE FIRST WEEK in April, in my part of the world at least, is a time when a man should take a good look at himself and the world and make a few private concessions to truth. There is no need for breast-beating and public confession of sin—we have had a plenty of that for now. What I am talking about is universal truth that is particularly obvious in the first few weeks of spring. March is too early, with spring still hovering beyond the next hill, and May is too late, with spring in possession of all the hills and valleys. But in early April a man can admit that he has nothing whatever to do with the opening of a bud or the sprouting of a seed. Spring is as independent of human management as sunrise or the phases of the moon.

Spring doesn't even abide by our mathematically meticulous almanacs. Neither do any of the other seasons, for that matter, but their deviations from what we call the norm are seldom so obvious. Last year we got a five-inch snowfall on the day of the vernal equinox. That is the kind of evidence of independence that I find difficult to ignore. True, I have seen hazelnut bushes in bloom in February, and I have found skunk cabbage thrusting its reptilian-looking snout through the ice in the bog in January. But neither of those incidents proves a thing except that the calendar is a human convenience, not a codification of natural law.

The emotional climate being what it is, I had a momentary twinge of conscience—I still can't quite bring myself to the point of calling it guilt—when I went down to the bog two weeks ago, the day of the equinox, and failed to hear the peepers. I half expected to hear the voluntary keepers of the national conscience say that I had to share the blame for this example of Hylaferous delinquency. But I didn't see a word about it in the papers the next day, so apparently they let that opportunity pass. Maybe they forgot about the equinox. I hope they did. I hope they will just let spring come in its own time and allow us to get on with the seasonal chores without feeling too totally guilty.

All winter we were bedeviled by their twinges of conscience. It seemed that every time we turned on the radio or television or picked up a newspaper or magazine, someone was saying we were guilty of something else. It was an old story, of course, but it seemed to be reaching pathological proportions. Actually, it went all the way back to Hiroshima and Auschwitz, and over the years we have all been saddled with an assortment of crimes, most of which I have no memory of either committing or even condoning in any sense. But we had become somewhat inured to it until somehow—I am still puzzled how—we were all made responsible for murder in Dallas. And after that we were saddled with responsibility for a list of crimes that ranged all the way from turmoil in Africa and Asia to poverty in every back street in America. From there it was only a short step to the verge of masochistic orgy, where even the obvious virtues were not only suspect but somehow reprehensible. As a countryman, I had no right to enjoy life as long as there were others who suffered injustice or deprivation anywhere. I, too, must suffer somehow, it seemed.

It was quite a winter, and I must say that at times some of us began to wonder what had happened to the national glandular system. Then, along in February, an article in the *Bulletin of the Atomic Scientists* gave a hint of what had been going on. It was a report by Hudson Hoagland, a pathologist and executive director of the Foundation for Experimental Biology at Worcester, Massachusetts. Hoagland was reporting on studies of the behavior and diseases of animals in overcrowded environments.

Hoagland's report tallied with a number of earlier reports that had less publicity. What they all add up to is that periodically, various animal species overpopulate their environments and succumb to maladies that are lumped under the term "acute stress syndrome." Physically, this syndrome appears as overactivity of the pituitary-adrenal system. This happens to be the glandular system that controls the release of hormones in time of stress. Animals that are stricken with it show evidence of liver disease, hypertension, atherosclerosis, and deterioration of the adrenals. In a majority of instances, animals that are so stricken die, even though they live in an environment with plenty of food and what would commonly be regarded as favorable factors except that it is overcrowded.

Hoagland's report cited a variety of animals and their symptoms. Minnesota jack rabbits were victims of liver and heart ailments. Rats showed abnormal social and sexual behavior. Deer sickened and died, often of glandular malfunction. White storks killed their own young.

Some years ago Durward Allen, a biologist with the Fish and Wildlife Service of the Department of the Interior, in a book called *Our Wildlife Legacy*, examined cycles in wildlife populations and came up with similar findings. Animal populations have cyclic rises and falls that appear to coincide, somewhat at least, with sunspot cycles. At times of most dense population, three factors kill them off—lack of food, epidemics of disease, and this same "acute stress syndrome," a kind of crowd-shock disease. Allen's research also showed that this stress syndrome affected the glandular system and was accompanied by liver and heart disease and a breakdown of the nervous system. He found that it occurred even when there was plenty of available food and when there were no more predators than usual. And he found, as Hoagland apparently found, that when the stress syndrome struck, the victims went into a kind of screaming-meemies state, were frightened of their own shadows, and even seemed to welcome violent death.

Then in 1964, Richard V. Rovbjerg, a zoology professor at the State University of Iowa, reported on research with crayfish, those little fresh-water crustaceans we used to call crawdads. They are pretty well down the scale of animal life, but Rovbjerg found that when crayfish overpopulate their environment they, too, get very jumpy. Their rather primitive nervous systems seem to go haywire, and they have the same kind of trouble that rabbits and rats and squirrels and deer and all the other animals have when they are forced to live in the midst of a crowd. In the report I have of Rovbjerg's findings I see no reference to the effect on the crayfish adrenal system, but it seems likely that the crawdads also suffer from glandular problems. They appear to have had the same kind of heart and liver trouble that all the other animals did, and they probably had hypertension too, though I'm not sure a crayfish would know whether his blood pressure was high or low.

Being scientists, none of these men goes so far as to say that what happens to animals inevitably happens to people. Hoagland does say that humans react pretty much the same way under stress and the pressures of overcrowding. He points out that other studies show that the human pituitary-adrenal system "responds under stress in a way similar to that of other animals." And he says that there is indirect evidence that inmates of concentration camps "experienced acute forms of the stress syndrome that may have accounted for many deaths."

So there it is. And if some of us wonder, from time to time, whether some of the more acute worriers and the most insistent breast-beaters aren't acting like over-crowded rabbits and crawdads, I don't think we are being too callous. Maybe our pituitaries don't react quite the way theirs do. I am not saying that they are already suffering from the acute stress syndrome, but most of them do seem to have quite a strong flow of adrenalin. If I were a physician, I would urge that they watch their blood pressure.

It may be, of course, that spring will help to ease things off. It won't be long now before a man can get outdoors, into a park if not into the open country, and see that the world doesn't consist entirely of four walls and a ceiling. The weather is going to warm up to a point where a man can even get a case of spring fever, if he will just let down a bit. In the old days, grandmother used to dose the family with sulphur and molasses and other elixirs to take the edge off spring fever, but in the present state of the world I think we would do well to encourage, not try to alleviate, that condition. A little vernal lethargy might do us all good.

As I was saying a few paragraphs back, the buds don't need any help or any worrying to achieve their own destiny. Maybe April was put in the calendar to demonstrate that. If man had never evolved, or if he were to vanish tomorrow, what happens in April would go right on happening simply because it is a consequence of natural forces that lie beyond man's reach. If it weren't for those forces, man wouldn't be here. I don't know what would be here, but this probably would be a planet as dead as the moon appears to be.

We were out in the garden the other morning preparing to plant peas, and I leaned on my fork for a moment and listened to the murmur of the brook that comes down off the mountain and across the home pasture. It was only the sound of flowing water, but it had all the music of spring in it. The grass along the brook was fresh and green, and only the day before I had seen bright, new leaves of violets there. While I stood there listening, when I should have been forking up the soil for the peas, I heard the red-winged blackbirds *O-ka-leeing*, and out in the pasture I saw a flock of robins working the grass and heard them chattering to each other.

A month ago the only sounds were the whistling of the chilly wind, the sighing of the trees, and the rather plaintively hopeful notes of chickadees and tree sparrows. A month from now the whole morning will be loud with bird song, the river will be in full flow, and the brook will be chattering day and night. The mountainside and pastures will be wholly green again, and the margins will be bright with wild flowers. Spring will be all around, and the earth will be waiting for the plow and the planter, but not demanding either. The first insects will be emerging from the egg and the pupa.

But right now it is April, and there is both promise and reassurance. Nothing, as far as I can see or hear, shows any signs of a bad conscience. I am sure that there were tragedies in the woods during the winter. A few trees were blown down, and a few deer died of privation or disease, and some of the birds were victims of weather and starvation. I hope that some of the insect hordes failed to survive, since I am a selfish creature with my own purposes and designs. But I see no evidence of remorse. True, I am a member of a species that is probably unique in possessing both conscience and compassion, but my kind also is endowed with a degree of what we call common sense. Maybe, now that April is here, some of the breast-beaters will come out and get a breath or two of fresh air and let their blood pressure subside.

Whether they do or not, that remnant of us who are still here close to the land will be hearing other voices. In the village the other morning all the talk I heard was about how much frost was still in the ground, how soon a man could get in to plow, and what kind of fertilizer to use on that lower forty. Somebody did mention that the President was still turning out the lights in the empty rooms, but that was the only reference to Washington. I might add that it was made with approval, although there was a grin behind it. Country folks have been turning out unneeded lights ever since they had to cart coal oil from town in a can with a cull potato stuck on the spout to keep it from splashing out.

It turned cold again the day after I forked up the ground for the peas, but we planted them just the same. Peas, like a good many other things, never grow unless you plant them, cold day or not. We put them in the ground and came in to warm our hands and get warmer jackets. Then we went out and raked some of the winter trash off the lawn. The chores have to be done, and a chilly day is a good time to get at them. As soon as it really warms up, I intend to go out and start getting a case of spring fever. I may even dig a few worms and go fishing. After the winter we've had, it will be good to sit on the riverbank in the sun and not feel guilty about anything.

1966—SUMMER

Summer and Belief

THE SOLSTICE past and July at hand, we have begun to relax and tell ourselves we never doubted that summer would come. But I must admit a twinge or two of skepticism when April seemed so unsure of itself. And when May brought snow instead of appleblossoms in its second week, I asked serious questions. I didn't actually look up the valley expecting to see an approaching ice sheet, but I was tempted to. If you can't believe in May and violets and appleblossoms, what can you believe in? I got my answer from a pair of brown thrashers, of all things.

I'm not a birdy-birdy man. Birds are birds, and I enjoy their color and song and thoroughly appreciate their help in keeping the insect hordes in check. Life would be miserable without them. But they aren't little feathered gnomes who think my kind of thoughts. However, I can accept the truth from a bird as wholeheartedly as Robert the Bruce did from a spider. Especially from a brown thrasher, whose sassy independence I thoroughly admire.

Normally the thrashers around here set up house-keeping in the untrimmed lilac bushes. But when they arrived this year the lilacs hadn't a leaf. None of the bushes or trees had except the willows, and the willow leaves were barely out of the bud. Baffled birds were all over the place, hungry for insects that hadn't hatched and without green shelter for nests. We kept the feeders stocked and put out extra suet, and we had more customers than a supermarket. But the brown thrashers were not among them. They rustled their own living somehow and even began gathering nesting materials, which seemed stupid to me. Birds shouldn't build nests and lay eggs in such weather.

The afternoon of May 10 it began to snow. We went out to see if it was real and at the far end of the front porch were greeted by such an outburst of hisses, squeals, and squawks as I had never heard. A pair of brown thrashers were warning us off from a big barberry bush where they had built a nest and laid two eggs.

The temperature fell into the twenties that night, but the next day there were three eggs, and the following day, four. Then the pair of them settled down to the job of hatching those eggs. And I decided that if those birds could believe in summer I could. I shifted my sights, let May take care of itself—it didn't do too badly in its second half, by the way—and we got the first cutting of hay in June, as always. The chances are that we will even get ripe tomatoes before killing frost comes again, probably early in September, maybe even in August.

Spring wasn't a perfect season, by any means, but it did lead to summer. I gave up expecting a perfect season long ago. A perfect day, yes, now and then, thanks to wind and weather and my own inner climate. Barbara, my wife, insists that weather is a state of mind anyway, and up to a point I agree. But not when I am at peace with the world and a late frost lays the garden low. Weather may be a consequence of cause and effect, but it isn't really rational.

But rationality, I have found, is relative and varies with the individual. It actually consists of a rather tenuous balance between romance and realism, between wish and fact. I was reminded of this in May when a bird-watcher friend stopped past after a record day with her field glasses.

As I said above, the weather had been difficult for the birds, particularly the migrants, who were caught in this area in unusual numbers. So our bird-watcher was triumphant. She exulted. But as we talked it became apparent that while she knew all the subtle variations of color and markings so important in identification, she knew almost nothing about what they eat, where they nest, how they mate, and the natural hazards they face. We mentioned that birds have parasites and said that nearly all of them are infested with lice. And she was not only astonished; she was hurt to the quick. "Phoebes do," she finally conceded. "But not orioles or cardinals or the really beautiful birds!"

We tried to ease her shock by saying that a few parasites don't dull the color or impair the songs, but she was not consoled. She didn't want her beautiful birds to have lice, and that's all there was to it. Which is what I mean by saying that we have varying degrees of rationality, of realism and romance. She didn't want lousy birds. I don't want lousy weather. But the fact is that few things are perfect in this world. If we were truly rational we would admit it and go on from there.

This won't be a perfect summer. We would get very tired of it if it were. July will bring hot days, warm nights, storms that will send thunder cannonading down the valley, evenings dusted with stars and alive with fireflies, whippoorwills whooping it up at three o'clock in the morning, and dawns to make a man remember his youth, when time had its proper dimensions. Or, to come closer to the truth, when man was still aware of time's dimensions.

The nearest thing to perfection that I know is a summer dawn. If you wanted to make one of those big, flat—and fallacious—statements, you might say that rural life persists just so that mankind won't forget the way a day begins. Such knowledge, I grant, won't feed the world's hungry, solve the China problem, get Vietnam on an even keel, or put a man safely on the moon. But it might help us to understand who we are, where we live, and what time it is, not by the clock or the calendar but by the stars and the earth on which we live.

I suspect that a midsummer dawn is so special because so few people are up and trying to manage or improve it. It is a tremendous happening in which man has no part except as an occasional fortunate witness. And it happens with neither haste nor confusion. The stars aren't hooked to a switch that turns them all off at once. The birds don't bounce out of bed and immediately start singing in unison. Darkness doesn't rise like a theatrical curtain and reveal the sun crouched like a sprinter ready to race across the sky.

I was up at four o'clock the other morning to go fishing before breakfast. First streaks of light were in the sky and the lesser stars had begun to dim when I got up, but I brewed a pot of coffee, had a first cup, filled a vacuum bottle, gathered bait and gear, and still had only half-light when I cast off my boat. By then the first birds were wakening and uttering first sleepy calls. But I went almost half a mile up the river before they really began to sing.

I had boated three fish before the full light of dawn, and even then the sun hadn't risen. Time was so deliberate that when I looked at my watch I thought it had stopped. I had been caught up in a different rhythm, one that seemed to have no relation to clocks. So I sat and watched and listened, and it was like seeing the earth emerge from the ancient mists. I was alone with creation; I and the birds who were in full voice now, a vast chorus of sheer celebration.

And at last came the silence, the hush—not a birdsong, not a rustled leaf. It was a kind of reverence, as though everything was awaiting the daily miracle. It lasted until the first ray of sunlight lit the treetops. Then the silence ended. The birds began to sing again, a vast jubilation. The sun had risen. A new day had begun. But it would be still another hour or two, until diurnal human beings were up and stirring, before the clock-driven haste would start all over again. Meanwhile, I had witnessed the deliberation of the dawn.

That is what I mean by perfection. Everything is right, at dawn. Nothing is hurried. Everything necessary to the day's beginning is in order and happening on its own schedule. Time is reduced to its true, eternal dimensions.

I came home an hour later, cleaned my fish, ate breakfast, and was back in conventional daylight time, which demanded that I go to work. I spent the morning at my desk, writing to meet a deadline, which is about as clockbound as a man can be. But I had somewhat restored my perspective, there on the river with the dawn. And that afternoon I wielded a hoe in the garden.

Working with the soil doesn't automatically endow a man with either wisdom or philosophy, but it does make him aware of orderly sequences such as night and day, summer and winter, bud, blossom, and seed. And of such certainties as life, death, and change. Knowing those things, a man can live with himself and probably get along with his neighbors.

Anyway, out there in the garden, waging war with the weeds, I began to feel, as I had at dawn, that things were fundamentally in order no matter what capers man was cutting. There wasn't any haste about growing things, which never try to take shortcuts. You can't order a seed to sprout by noon tomorrow. All you can do is go along with the season and the sequence. As Albert, my neighbor down the road, said when he was planting corn in weather that demanded a winter coat and a cap with ear flaps, "If you don't get the seed in the ground it sure won't grow." He wasn't being a philosopher; he was just being a practical realist. And now the corn he planted that frosty day is just about at the stage the corn was a year ago. He put the seed in the ground, and it grew, in its own time.

A good many things have changed about country life in the past fifty years, but the old sequences and inevitabilities still prevail. You can't cancel them, and you ignore them at your own peril. You have to believe in them.

Last winter we had to cut one of the big sugar maples. An old lightning scar left a wound that eventually rotted out the heart and made the tree a hazard to the power lines. So we cut it down and made enough firewood to last ten years; a poor bargain, firewood for a living tree, but the best we could make. And one mild day I went out and counted the growth rings in the stump. There were ninety-six, which put that tree's sprouting back around 1870. But the important thing about those rings was the continuity. They varied with the years, some broad, some narrow, as the tree grew or languished with the seasons, but there were no gaps. That old tree never skipped a year, early spring or late, wet summer or dry. And cripple though it was, had we let it stand it would have added still another ring this summer.

That's what I mean by the sequence and the continuity: growth, the persistence of life, whether it is a blade of grass or a towering sugar maple. The seed sprouts, the stem grows, buds take form, and blossoms open.

Blossoms make seed and the cycle is repeated, seed to root and stem, flower to seed, over and over, unending. The seed and the egg, one and the same, fundamentally, the germ of life whether it is a daisy or an oak, a butterfly or a man.

What can a man believe in? I suppose it depends on what a man is looking for, but I know that if you watch a nesting bird and experience a midsummer dawn you can't fail to believe in something. Life and time, if nothing else. Given those, almost anything is possible that a rational man might want.

1966–AUTUMN

October and Answers

FIRST FROST came on one of those still, star-shot nights of late September, and I wakened at three o'clock in the morning, lay listening and wondered what had happened. The quiet was so deep that the only sound I heard was the throb of my own pulse against the pillow. I held my breath, listening for the insect chorus that had been a part of the night since May, and there wasn't even a scratch against the darkness. Then I heard the rustle of the leaves in the big apple tree, and a moment later a red fox barked on the hillside. I let out my held breath and heard the faint echo of a barred owl hooting from across the valley. Then I went back to sleep reassured. Autumn had come, and the quiet, but not The Silence.

To waken in the night and hear the quiet of autumn for the first time can be a startling experience. You have seen a change coming, the subtle shift of noonday shadows, the weary look of the leaves in the elms, the first drift of milkweed floss, and you have felt the change in the look and feel of the air itself. But not until you lie in the darkness and hear no cricket, no katydid, not one of the little sounds that are the proclamation of teeming, transient life, are you aware of the possibility of silence; and to know that there can be no silence, summer or winter, so long as there is life on earth, is an awesome realization. You are here, sentient, listening, waiting. Are you alone? Then comes the relief of hearing a rustled leaf, a fox, an owl—of knowing that it is the first, frosty quiet of autumn, nothing more. Your pulse quiets, your mind banishes the specter, and you sleep again, confident of tomorrow.

I slept, and dawn came, sunrise, a chilly morning with white frost on the outbuilding roofs. The sun climbed, warmed the air, and all the vines and tender plants in the garden sagged and blackened. The cold front had passed through, but its mark was indelible. Barbara looked out the kitchen window and said, "Now the final hoarding." We went out to complete the harvest. Not much, for we had made the major harvest several days before, but there were a few winter squashes now revealed among the wilted vines, a peck or so of late limas on the blackened stems, one last picking from the late planting of sweet corn. And we bade farewell to the tomatoes.

By then it was mid-morning, and I found a fat bumblebee sunning itself on a shaggy orange zinnia in which it had sheltered for the night, still so arthritic it had to soak up sunlight half an hour before it could fly. In the garden path half a dozen big black ants crept about like rheumatic old men, seeking sun-warmed spots to rest and ease their joints. On the stepping stone at the woodshed door a woolly bear caterpillar slowly uncurled and tried to reach the crack beneath the door, looking for a place to hibernate.

Albert, our dairy-farmer neighbor, stopped on his way up the road and said, "A good frost clears the air. Now we'll have a spell of fair weather. Down to twenty-five at my house this morning!" He didn't say it, but we knew he was glad, as we were, to have a proper end to summer and the growing season. On the land you live by the seasons and it is good to have them clearly defined, not by the calendar but by the weather. And first frost is one of the necessary markers.

Autumn was here, October at hand. But no cycle ends abruptly or completely. We gathered and stowed, and by noon I heard a cricket chirping in the compost heap. By mid-afternoon two Monarch butterflies were playing tag in the dooryard. And by evening a few katydids were stridulating, slowly and with a tired rasp but alive and making noise. Summer's tag ends remained, though the hoarding was under way all around us.

The ant and the honeybee, as everybody knows, are provident even in human terms—they gather and stow food for the winter. But even those we think of as improvident also hoard. The loud ones as well as the silent ones, the scratchers and stridulators as well as the quiet creepers and crawlers, hoard life. They commit life to the egg, where it will outlast the long, cold, hungry days and renew itself next summer and all the summers to come. Once life is so committed, hoarded in the egg, the insect's individual span nears its end and the fiddling and the scratching are little more than the instinctive proclamation that even ebbing individual life persists. We all proclaim the same thing, one way or another. If our human lives were shortened to one summer in the sun we too, no doubt, would make much of senile complaints in our autumn. But there are various rules, and we, knowing many summers, abide by a different one—we harvest and hoard, cherish individual life and provide as best we can for its full span.

Spring is sprouting, summer is growth, and autumn is ripeness and completion. If I am wise, I watch the trees, the birds, the animals and the insects and somewhat learn from them, for they are all a part of the same vast reservoir of life in which I participate. The maples hoard their sap, shed their leaves and prepare for winter, rest, and, in a sense, consolidation. The oaks ripen acorns and the wild grape ripens seeds within the purple fruit, hostages to their species-future, then trust them to bird and beast to plant at random in the unknowing certainty that acorns and grape seeds will sprout, in due season, and perpetuate their kind.

The woodchucks in my back pasture hoard fat beneath their tawny pelts, clean out their dens, and prepare to hoard their spark of life through a long sleep that verges on death. The chipmunks line their tunnel-nests with grass and down, pack their granaries with small nuts and seeds, and settle down to outlast the ice and darkness. Flicker and thrasher and robin fly south, but jays hoard acorns, grouse fatten and feather their legs and feet, chickadees choose evergreen shelter, sparrows claim weed patches that will not be drifted over completely. Ducks find inlets that will be ice-free.

One way and another, they hoard and protect life that it may continue, in the seed, in the egg, in the individual.

I sometimes think that autumn is the best time of all to look for meanings. Not for reasons, which probably will remain mysteries as long as man is here to wonder, but for the shape of life and possibly its purpose, just possibly. I went out the other afternoon and looked at a leaf, an acorn, a blue jay's feather, a dead beetle, an opening milkweed pod.

It was a yellow maple leaf, freshly fallen. A dead leaf, discarded by the tree, a sheet of cellulose now bright with carotene where mysterious green chlorophyll was at work a month ago. A leaf that breathed, had a pulse of sap in its veins, transmuted sun and moisture into starch that fed the parent tree. A maple leaf, shaped to its kind and yet not precisely the same as any other leaf that ever grew. Now waste, discard, the substance of leaf mold to feed future root and stem and leaf. A life shape, now lifeless.

A squirrel was busy in the nearby oak, and its scurry shook an acorn from its cup. It rolled down the slope to where I stood and I held it in my hand, round, smooth, packed, a life-germ and the food to nourish its sprouting. Was it round to help it roll beyond the old oak's shade and to a better seedbed? Or round because of all shapes the sphere and the ovoid have the greatest possible capacity? In it was life, the very shape of a leaf, a tree, perhaps the dream of tomorrow's oak. If so, whose dream?

The feather was recently shed, perhaps moulted and already replaced but still bright with color. Intricate beyond duplication except by the bird itself, it was almost weightless. Perhaps in a remote yesterday it was a reptile scale that became a feather to launch a changing life form into the freedom of the air. Like the leaf, dispensable; and like the leaf a life-shape now lifeless.

The beetle I found was of the scarab family, kin of ancient Egypt's sacred scarabs, but when I found it, it was an empty chitin carapace from which the bronze tones of life had faded, leaving only a dull black husk. Big as my fingerend, it weighed only a small fraction of an ounce. It looked complex as some miniature machine, with stiff legs, intricate claws, vacant eyes, open mandibles; yet it was only an empty box with strange appendages. The inner tissues and the juice of life were gone. It once was something that hatched, fed, crawled; changed from soft grub to encapsulated pupa; achieved inadequate wings, complex legs, fierce mandibles; mated, laid eggs, died—all while I was noting time only from one equinox to another. Now there was nothing but this thin, horny shell, a life-shape from which life had seeped away like water from a leaky pail. Its kind were here long before my kind, and to the old Egyptians it was a symbol of resurrection and immortality. Whose immortality? This shell I held in my hand was the shape of life but no longer live, the miracle of life once lived and now gone elsewhere, committed to the hidden egg.

The milkweed pod was shaped like cupped hands now open, a silk-lined womb where life had matured its seeds. My fingers had to touch its lining, feel the texture, smooth as the floss-tufts that bore the ripe seeds down the wind in a shimmering mist. The last few seeds drifted away at the touch of a finger, and the empty pod was a silent memory of summer-blossom, fragrance, bee-hum, dew, rain, sunlight, and the potency of pollen, the readiness of the egg, their fertile union. It was summer matured into autumn, life risen from root to leaf to bud, to blossom, to swelling pod; life entrusted to the fluff-borne seeds to go elsewhere and sprout and rise again from root to pod, over and over and over again.

I plucked the empty pod and carried it home, an autumn insigne. And that evening, as I have said, I heard the tired rasping of a few katydids like dying echoes of late August.

But I had lain and listened to the quiet, the night before, and I had my reassurance. Everywhere I turned that day I found the substance of the meaning, which is change and flow. Natural change, inevitable flow, which can no more be cancelled than sunlight or stargleam. With every breath, I partake of it. With every throb of my pulse.

Last summer a man whose technical knowledge I respect said to me, "We are not far from the big breakthrough." I asked, "Breakthrough into what?" And he said, "The big answers. Life, space, the universe." And I said, "There they are, all three of them. What further answer do we need?" And he talked of genes, nucleic acid, heredity, and ways to manage and control. He would have gone on about rockets and interplanetary messengers, but I said, "Management and control are not answers—they are techniques." And I took him to the garden and showed him a cabbage plant infested with aphids among which a dozen ants were making their rounds.

I tried to explain about aphids and parthenogenesis, which he vaguely understood. Then I explained how ants manage and control aphids, milking them for a sweet food they make and exude. Not being a naturalist, he did not quite understand this, but he accepted it. He accepted, that is, until I pointed out that ants, with only a slight trace of what we know as intelligence, learned to manage and control long before man evolved and still, eons later, are ants. And I asked, "Can your techniques create an ant? Or an aphid? Or endow them with intelligence?"

"Why should we?" he asked. "To what purpose?"

"They are a part of life," I said. "How can you give me the answers to life without giving me the answer to an aphid?"

"Can an aphid, or even an ant, orbit a rocket?" he asked.

That ended our conversation. To the technician, techniques are the sum, the substance, and answers consist of data. But I wondered, the other day, if my technical friend wakened in the night, as I did, and heard the quiet and wondered about The Silence. Probably not. Or if he did, he thought of the quiet in terms of decibels, not of life.

But now, with the glory of the woodlands spreading over the hills and with ripeness and achievement all around us, life is more insistent than data. Life, which creates the leaf for its own purpose, and the nut, the floss-blown seed, the ephemeral beetle. Everywhere I turn are the insignia, complex and various beyond comprehension, of the shape life takes; of the vast stream of life that flooded the earth all summer, green with chlorophyll, red with hemoglobin, throbbing, breathing, growing, and now is hoarded in a thousand different ways. And I partake. I, like any countryman, hoard the substance and sustenance of life, knowing that my harvest is a way of living. One way.

Right now, hearing a cricket chirp, hearing a crow caw, seeing a flurry of leaves from the big elm across the lawn, I know that management and control are not the answer. I heard the only answer I can comprehend or accept the other night, when first hard frost came and brought the quiet. When I lay listening, and knew that I was not alone.

January and the Totals

THE GEESE came early, but killing frost was late, so it was anybody's guess about the winter. But as Morris said the day we watched the geese, "High as they fly, I doubt that even geese can see the weather two months ahead." So I guessed that it would be cold by Christmas, snowy by New Year's Day, and we would hear the peepers in April. I stand by that, especially the peepers.

It was the last week in October when the geese arrived. We were down at the lake getting things in hand after a vicious autumn storm that swamped my small boat at its mooring. The outboard motor got a bath, so I brought it home and dried it out, and that day we were trying it out. We bailed out the boat, mounted the motor on the transom, and were just gassing up when I heard the clamor. It was like the distant barking of small dogs, a whole pack of them. We looked up, searching the sky, and Morris said, "Geese!" They came in low over the hill to the north, just above the treetops, so close I could hear the whistling of their wings.

They knew where they were going, for they didn't circle even once. They came right in, big wings cupped, long necks outstretched, webbed feet splayed, and struck the water with a rush of spray. There were more than a hundred of them, Canadas, with white chin-straps gleaming and heads and necks jet black. We watched as they spread out and set their sentinels, two big old ganders, and we listened to their chatter; for it was chatter, not the gabbling flight talk you can hear a mile away. Maybe they were talking about the lake, old ones telling youngsters that it is off-limits for hunters, so they could relax. Or maybe they were swapping gossip with the dark little bob-tailed grebes—we call them hell-divers—that had put an end to our perch fishing. Whatever they were saying, they settled down as though they had a three-months lease.

I pulled out the choke, turned the motor over a few times, and it caught. The dunking hadn't hurt it. Morris grinned at me and shoved off. We went around the margin of the lake a little way, then headed for the geese to have a closer look. The old sentinel ganders stretched their necks, swam toward us, and honked a warning to the flock. But they didn't take wing. They were tired. They must have come a long way. We circled them, respectfully distant, made a rough count, then went back to my dock and stowed the motor in my cabin. A haze had begun to gather in the sky, the kind of haze that can mean snow but sometimes means

Indian Summer. That was when Morris said he doubted that the geese could see the weather ahead.

It didn't snow, but it turned raw and blustery. We had hoped for another chance or two to troll deep for the big trout, but a week later we gave up. The spray had coated the dock with ice and I almost went head over heels into five feet of water cold enough to freeze a seal's flippers. So we took in the boat, stowed our rods and said, "That's that, till April." It was only the first week in November, but late autumn was upon us, winter just ahead. The year was fraying out like the thistleheads in the back pasture.

A few days later we were up on my mountainside looking for partridges. The leaves had all fallen from everything but the oaks, but the rain hadn't settled them; walking through the woods was like walking around in a giant box of cornflakes. We found the birds, but they heard us coming and were gone in a roar before we got within a hundred yards of them. We had a good climb and saw a fine assortment of red and brown and purple oaks, and we didn't fire a shot.

I read the other day that some architect, obviously not one of those who build towering, windowless boxes, had said that man, even in an urbanized environment, needs "the vital stimulus of shifting light, passing time, and the changing of the seasons." Maybe that is why we countrymen insist on living where we do. Not for the fishing or the partridges we sometimes hunt, but for that vital stimulus. Maybe that is why we don't look on winter as such a dour, forbidding season. We see the light shift, are constantly aware of passing time, and are a living part of the changing seasons. We don't have to look at the calendar or the almanac to know what time it is. We don't even have to look out the window. We just know it in our bones, maybe the way the geese do. I sometimes wish I was as wise as a wild goose.

By then, of course, we had to catch up with the seasonal chores. You have to prepare for winter, even if gasoline and electricity do take most of the back-breaking labor out of rural life today. They can't do your thinking for you. They don't respond to that vital stimulus. Turn a wheel or close a switch and they run, summer or winter. So we took in the late harvest, snugged the buildings, protected the water lines, checked the barnyard fences, made sure the roofs were tight. And those of us who like the comfort of an open fire or a wood stove in the kitchen for those middling days when it's too warm for a wool shirt and muffler, not warm enough for shirtsleeves, made sure the wood pile was amply stocked.

Ed, my neighbor up the road, sold off his cows. "At my age," he said, "barn chores get to be a burden in the winter." Ed has farmed that place for more than forty years, tending cows every day of all that time. He has laid away a competence, as they say, and earned a rest. But one man's rest is another man's labor, I suppose. A newcomer from the city who is building what he calls a retirement place twenty miles from here spotted Ed's old barn last summer and made him an offer for the hand-hewn beams. Up here, when we build a new house we want it new, but there are those who want a new house old to begin with, maybe thinking they can buy memories and old traditions that way. Anyway, Ed sold his cows and spent most of the fall taking the sheathing off his barn to get at those beams. He saved the sheathing, too, took all the nails out, and stacked it carefully. That was his idea of taking a rest. No doubt he will sell those old boards, too, to someone who wants his brand new living room to look like an old barn turned inside out.

November passed, with a little snow that didn't stay on the ground and with rain that refreshed the springs. And with more Christmas merchandising than I can remember so early in the season. Someone suggested that we just cancel Thanksgiving and get Christmas over with early, which might have been a good idea, at that. But you can't sell Christmas like a truckload of old beams, and you can't swap Thanksgiving for Christmas. Not in New England. Thanksgiving is one antique that is not for sale at any price. So we roasted the turkey right on schedule, mashed the yellow turnips, creamed the onions, made the mince pies, and said our thanks not for excess but for plenty, not for privileges but for opportunities and obligations. For health and strength and the persistent dream of justice and peace.

Regardless of the calendar, December is the shortest month. It has the shortest days, in terms of daylight, and those days are far too few for what has to be done. Morris works for the power company and we saw him several times, but only momentarily; he was patrolling the back roads with his crew, keeping the lines in order. After one sleety storm he stopped in just long enough to say, "I guess I was wrong about those geese.

They saw it coming." Then he was gone again, looking for an ice-wracked tree down across the wires.

December. Firelight and greens and a tree from our own mountainside. The crèche in the village churchyard. Carols. The Christmas eve service. Ribbons and tinsel and gay wrappings. The messages from far away. And the remembering. The friendship tokens, which add the humanity, the from-the-heart sense of being, and lift the holy season out of the caves of Mammon at least toward the miracle of belief. We are a long, long way from Bethlehem, but on Christmas Day itself we know that the bells we hear are not ringing in either Sodom or Gomorrah.

The winter solstice, and Christmas, and here we are in the midst of winter, any way you look at it. Daylight begins to lengthen, though you need a sextant and a chronometer to prove it. The next full moon won't occur until January 26th, which means that nights now are dark as well as long. The icy fang of the winter bites deep. The owls are loud and the fox barks on the hillside, reminding the restless sleeper how quiet is the night when the year turns on its silent axis. The ice booms on the river, and the lake echoes with its expansion cracks. Snow whines underfoot. The wind whistles in the pines, the boreal hunter summoning the hounds of ice-bound hunger.

The year sums up its seasons in the dormant trees, the flown bird, the hibernating woodchuck. And man, neither plant nor bird but sentient animal whose blood can freeze as easily as water, survives. That, in a sense, is his own summary—man survives. With less sense than a wild goose, in some ways; with less stamina than wolf, less cunning than a fox, he still persists.

We draw up our totals, out of sheer habit, totting up all the inconsequentials, for our own pride and for the tax collector. Another year, we say, thinking thus to tie it neatly in a bundle like so many old newspapers. Then we look out, we countrymen at least, and see the hills and we wonder, "What is another year?" You can't take time like an endless cord and tie knots in it and say, "Now I own this much." The cord has slipped through your fingers, knots and all, before you can count up to a hundred, even as we used to do, cheating a bit, as children playing hide and seek: "Ten, ten, double-ten, forty-five, fifteen." There are no short-cuts swift enough to stop the flow of time.

But we do the summing up, hopeful, reaching for certainty, perhaps for reassurance. And the sums are all wrong, because there are no totals. We are a part of the only total, and all our numbering is but finger-counting.

I was out in the back pasture the other morning, booted and mufflered and breaking through the snow crust at every step. For a few minutes I thought I had found a summary in the snow itself. It was the summary of snowflakes, of ice-crystals, that fell from the clouds last week. Then I came to a big rock, the one we call the Resting Rock because we go there to sit and rest, at peace with our intimate world, in summer. And there I found where the sun had warmed the south side of the rock and melted the snow. The summary of the flakes had vanished, oozed away into the ground, and left only a scum of ice. Then I looked at the rock itself, a big old boulder brought here maybe ten thousand years ago by the ice sheet. And there was another summary, of geologic forces and basic substances. But again, an incomplete summary, for it was a part of something far greater, worn and shaped by the ice and the journey.

I went on, and at the fence row I saw the naked trees, the birches and maples and sapling ash, and the undergrowth of hazel brush. All of them had summed up their summers, one way or another, in growth rings and leaves and seeds or nuts. But what is a seed, a nut, but a promise of tomorrow, another year, more growth, more seeds, endlessly? Time flows over and through even the trees as insistently, as ceaselessly, as the wind.

And I saw the tracks of a rabbit, a fox, two field mice. I heard a cardinal whistle and a jay scream. Warm blood, like mine. Flesh, like mine, that quivers with pain. Senses keener than mine. And I thought how they, too, if they could count as I do, might try to summarize, and fail. Or perhaps, being in some ways more practical than my own kind, might not bother to summarize, knowing how useless are numbers in the face of infinity. Whatever this is, we are all in it, and the numbers can't define or explain it.

I came back to the house, the outsize carapace man invented when he accepted the fact that he couldn't hibernate like the turtle. It was a warm house, thanks to fire. And I thought wryly of the friend who insists that man's great discovery wasn't how to build a fire, but how to put out the flame. Otherwise, he says, man would have burned himself to death before he even dreamed of civilization. I came into the house and had a hot drink to warm my blood and bones, and I knew I was right in my forecast, back there in October. I wasn't as smart as the geese, but I suspected it would be cold by Christmas and snowy by New Year's. And I said we would hear the peepers in April. I still stand by that.

1967—SPRING

The Root, the Seed, the Egg

WINTER apparently ended just in time. The way we heard it, another foot of snow would have put New York, Chicago, and maybe another dozen major cities out of business. For a while, megalopolitan civilization hung in the balance with all its atom-smashing, jet-propelled promises of an Elysian tomorrow. It was saved only by plodding men using machines and methods of snow-removal that haven't changed much since World War II. And, though nobody mentioned it, by seasonal inevitability. The savage tooth of winter was dulled by lengthening daylight, which all the computers couldn't hasten or delay by one micro-second. The fact remained that even in the cities snow and ice eventually melt and seldom long outlive the vernal equinox.

Meanwhile, the weather was somewhat on our conscience as we went on safely living here in the rural hills, our roads plowed out, our paths shoveled, our heat and light still functioning, even our contacts with the outside world in working order and bringing us, every hour, word of urban trials and tribulations. I won't admit more than a slight trace of smugness, but some of us did wonder if the wave of the future was carrying all of us into such a predicament. Maybe, we thought, it was just as well to drag our heels a little longer, until the technicians either devise a way to cope with weather as effectively as their grandfathers did or temper their boasts of omnipotence. It's hard to believe in miracles when the miracle workers have to put down their magic wands and reach for an old-fashioned snow shovel.

Johnny, my dairy-farmer neighbor up the road, pretty well summed it up when he plowed out my driveway after the season's heaviest snowfall. "Can't fight the weather," he said. "About all you can do is dig out and plow out and hope for an early spring. Besides," he added, "we do need the moisture."

So we dug out and plowed out and went on living with the weather, doing the daily chores and watching the daylight lengthen, knowing that the vernal equinox would come, right on schedule. The ice went out of the river, the ducks came back, we heard the geese honking high as they arrowed north in the moonlight, and we listened for the spring peepers. The slow, eternal change began to rouse life down at the root. Maple sap flowed soon after Washington's birthday, as usual; and I don't know a more reassuring event than sap-rise. It comes to the hillside maple groves while the drifts still lie cold and crunchy in the woodland, and we always think that if sap can rise in the maples, hope can surely hold on in the human heart a few weeks longer.

Sap-rise, of course, means that winter dormancy is

approaching its end. It means that the incredible surge of life, the infinite fecundity of nature, will soon be evident again in its seasonal cycle. Back in January and February, every time it snowed I thought about infinity as I watched the swirling flakes. There aren't numbers enough to count the flakes that fall on the roof of my house, let alone those that fall on my pastures. But the infinity of snowflakes is cold and inert. For all their crystalline perfection and complexity, snowflakes cannot grow or reproduce themselves. They overwhelm me only with countless numbers.

Then the peepers yelp in the lowlands and the pussy willows cautiously open their fuzzy male catkins. The peepers mate and lay their masses of minute, gelatinous eggs in the chilly water. The inconspicuous female willow flowers reach their receptive stage and the silky catkins ripen their yellow pollen. Infinitesimal flecks of life are all around me, on the wind, in the water. The willows achieve fertile seeds. The batrachian eggs hatch into tiny, wriggling tadpoles. Neither are as countless as the snowflakes, but still are far beyond counting, life incredibly resurgent. And, in the untold eons of springtime since the first frogs mated in the primal swamplands and the somewhat fewer eons since trees began strewing pollen on the marshy margins, perhaps as countless as the snowflakes of all the winters I shall ever know.

Only now and then are we really aware of this amazing procreative force, but when we do see it it is like a glimpse of the big, enduring secret. A few years ago we saw it on a warm spring evening.

The peepers called, mated, and laid their eggs. So

did all the other toads and frogs that populate the riverbanks just beyond my dooryard. Mild weather came and held. To me, it was only ideal weather for farm crops and revitalizing for winter-weary people. But the miracle was happening on my very doorstep. Then came the mild evening when we walked up the road close beside the river to know the smell of opening buds, the leaf-mold scent that comes with the stir of worms and the thrust of new grass. It was early darkness and I had a flashlight in case a leisurely shadow might be a foraging skunk looking for a late supper. I have found that a flashlight beam will delay a startled skunk's reaction long enough for a watchful walker to retreat to safety.

We walked a little way and suddenly sensed that the whole road was alive. Unseen creatures were moving all around us. I turned on the flashlight and in its beam were countless hordes of small frogs and toads, a seething carpet of them as far up the road as I could see. They were like a scourge of locusts on the march, but they were only moving from the riverbank across the road and into the open pastureland beyond.

We stood there and they were all around us, underfoot and blindly leaping at our legs and over our feet. Barbara exclaimed, "I don't believe it! There aren't that many frogs in the world!" It seemed that the river, wide as it was, could not possibly have held so much amphibian life as was carpeting that country road. We watched for ten minutes, and still they came. We turned and came back to the house, scufflling our feet to push the frogs out of our way.

I went out again an hour later, and while the mass migration had ended there were still dozens of small toads and frogs crossing the road from riverbank to pasture. But by the next morning there wasn't one in sight, and when I walked out into the pastures I didn't find a toad or frog. Those untold thousands that had spawned in the river, unknown to me, had migrated across my consciousness by mere chance, there in the darkness, and vanished completely. Yet I doubt that what I saw was a phenomenon of fecundity. It probably happens every spring. I merely saw it for the first time. But, thinking about it later, I remembered the kangaroo rats.

We had been to the West Coast, some years ago, and were driving home; late one afternoon I left the main highway in western Kansas to look for the little known ruins of an obscure outpost of the Indian wars. A thundercloud was rising, black and threatening, but we were on a good gravel road and with luck we would see the ruins and be in Garden City by dark. Within ten miles, however, my luck ran out. We came to a place where the road was being rebuilt just as the thunderstorm built up to a cloudburst. The freshly graded road became a greasy strip of gumbo between two perilous ditches. We never found the old ruins, and darkness caught us thirty miles north of Garden City.

Then my luck returned. We came to a hard-packed sandy road and the storm passed. Tired and hungry, I began to hurry; but within another mile I was aware of strange activity at the roadside and slowed up again. The bare, sandy shoulder of the road had become a raceway and playground for kangaroo rats, literally thousands of them, lured out by the rain and the cool darkness. They leaped and frolicked and raced and seemed almost to dance in the beams of the car's headlights. They were Ord's kangaroo rats, native to the sandy areas of the Great Plains, glistening orange-brown on the back, gleaming white on the belly, with big, dark eyes and long, tufted tails. Thousands, did I say? Hundreds of thousands, rather; perhaps millions. For more than ten miles we idled along that road, fascinated. Then they were gone. We drove on in to Garden City and found food and shelter.

But when I asked the room clerk if they often saw the kangaroo rats he looked at me as though I were crazy. "Rats?" he said, brusquely defensive. "There aren't any rats around here." And the next morning when I asked the same question of the man at the filling station he said that a friend of his once caught a kangaroo rat and kept it in a cage for a while, but it died. That was the only one he ever saw. And he asked, with a grin, "Sure those weren't grasshoppers you saw? We grow 'em pretty big around here, and there's a lot this year out on that road." I didn't argue. Most of us live unaware in the midst of teeming life.

April isn't the time to see most of that life, but it is the time of beginnings. And by late April the midges are out, the first of those miniature hordes that no countryman can ignore. So tiny that one common name for them is No-Seeums, they swarm in every patch of vegetation and cloud the air that the outdoor worker breathes. Count them? It would be easier to count leaves!

And by April's end the first pollen of the season after the willows is dusting the air wherever conifers grow. Last spring when I went to my dentist's office he impatiently swept his hand across the polished top of an instrument case, held it out to me and asked, "Where does all that yellow dust come from? It gets all over everything every year at this time." I ran a finger across the cabinet, looked at the golden gleam of minute particles and asked, "Where are the nearest pines?"

"Pines?" he asked. "Pine trees?" He pointed to a row of big, old white pines fifty yards away. "What have they got to do with it?"

"It's pine pollen," I told him. The pollen from those pines was dusting the grass and sifting into every house for several hundred yards around. I couldn't say how much pollen those pines were spilling into every breeze, but I know it was beyond human comprehension.

We have, close beside our own house, one towering old Norway spruce, and every spring its male catkins fill the air with pollen. The air shimmers in the sunlight for days. And on the front porch, where the breezes eddy, that pollen settles in drifts and ripples. I sweep it up, at the peak of pollen time, to keep from tracking it into the house, and I often get half a pint of it. How much pollen is there in half a pint, how many grains? That spruce pollen, like the pollen from the white pines, is finer than dust. I can barely make out the shape of the individual grains under a ten-power glass. When I try to guess I have to say there are more pollen grains on my front porch than there were snowflakes on my front lawn all last winter. And every one of those grains of pollen is a fleck of life.

Life. We are dealing with life, in frog eggs, in gnats, in pollen grains. And we are dealing with infinity, as far as we can judge; certainly with numbers beyond our human comprehension. We are dealing with spring, and life renewing itself. How can anyone be unaware? The seed, the egg, the root—awakening and each one with its own degree of sentience, its own response. The earth's axis moves a trace, the sun's rays are a hair less slanted, the air warms by a few degrees, and things happen. We see a migrant robin, watch a maple tree burst bud, follow a hungry bee from one crocus to another. Spring comes, we say. Winter is over and gone, and now life will be easier for another season, with no snow to clog the streets, no ice to choke the harbors. We have won through another winter. We have survived.

And all around us is proof that life survives, teeming life of which we are only a minor manifestation. And the miracles are in the root, the seed, the egg, not in the laboratories or the machines. The enduring truth of the earth, and perhaps of the universe, is implicit in April —in springtime.

July and Reality

LOOKING BACK NOW, it seems impossible that our spring was so late, so cold, so wet. Even city folk, to whom such weather is primarily a week-end inconvenience, resented it; and here in the country we kept seasonal schedules with difficulty. We did get the spring plowing done, and the planting; but we don't expect to have to wear winter mittens while planting corn. The point, though, is that now things have pretty well evened out. It is summer on the land as well as in the almanac, and despite the late spring we weren't overwhelmed by chaos and senseless futility. The earth kept spinning, the seasons did follow their eternal sequence, and the urge to sprout and grow didn't even falter. The forces that run this earth maintained fundamental order and system even in the face of difficulties, including human doubt and disillusionment.

I am prompted to this reminder by the pronouncement, back in April, by one of the more moderate critics of life and art. "It is human nature," he said, "to want every package to be tidy. Loose ends make us nervous. . . . But the tidy package is a vanishing luxury. Life," he summed up, "is becoming so complex that it contains no easy solutions."

I read that during one of our dour, discouraging weeks of reluctant spring, but even then I wondered what life he was talking about, what loose ends were making me nervous, what tidy packages now were so rare. I put on a coat, went out, and life all around me, even at that tentative stage, was about as tidily packaged as I could imagine. If anyone can create a neater package than the bud on a maple or a dogwood, I would like to see it. A hickory bud, I will admit, looks rather disorganized when the bud scales open and that silky membrane is torn apart, but as leaves, blossoms, and tender shoots emerge I am always filled with awe at the neatness and economy with which the astonishing bud is packed.

And there were practically no loose ends in sight. Last fall there was a bit of jumble when the leaves fell in absolute disorder and empty milkweed pods, goldenrod stems, and wild carrot heads made jackstraw tangles at roadsides and in fencerows. But winter's snows smoothed things out, and by April all that disorderly discard was turning to leaf mold and humus. What looked like the tag ends of the year last November turned out to be April's ideal rootbed for new life. Spring, the rootbed of summer itself, was about as tidy a package as one could wish for. Complex, yes, but still tidy because it was purpose being fulfilled.

I decided that the oracular critic was wrong on at least two major points. He was indulging in *homo men-*

sura, the all-too-common habit of mistaking personal confusion for universal disorder. And he was out of step with the seasons. Periodically we have to endure the autumn and winter of the emotions, littered with disillusionment and alienation; but eventually that litter becomes the rootbed for another spring, in ourselves, and the maturity of another summer. That critic was still back in November, unaware in the midst of change.

It sometimes seems that the simplest truths are the most difficult to understand and accept. I don't know why unless it is that we prefer to talk rather than listen. Maybe we should more often, particularly in May or June, spend an hour on a hillside or in a meadow and renew contact with basic realities. Not talking about them, but listening to them, letting them seep into us. Listening, not so much with our ears but with our awareness; for most of this earth's work is accomplished very quietly. Nothing is less audible than the growth of grass, the process of photosynthesis in a woodland's leaves, the pollination of a blossom, the quickening of life in an egg. And few accomplishments are more strictly ordered, more committed to sequence and completion.

At the height of spring, early or late, I can walk across my pastures or sit on a sun-warm rock in an opening in the mountainside woodland, and know that there is both order and meaning all around me. Merely by being there, I am a participant—simply by acknowledging that I am a part of life, not the whole of it, I accept the fact of order and system. I become aware of things beyond myself, of the whole environment which fostered my own kind and thus far has perpetuated it.

Perhaps if I could forget such an apparently minor but ultimately marvelous and mysterious a thing as a seed I, too, could think of life as senseless and chaotic. But that would mean that I must forget all the yesterdays, all the beginnings, both remote and immediate, that add up to here and now. How can I, or anyone with eyes to see and any degree of understanding, forget to that degree? Out there in the pasture or on that old rock, yesterdays and beginnings are all around me, implicit not in me but in life itself. I don't have to go back to the cycads to recognize an oak tree and know that it grew from an acorn. I don't have to recapitulate the evolution of the lung to know that both frogs and toads are hatched as tadpoles. I don't even have to date the last ice sheet to know that a glacier carved this valley. All I have to know, to accept, is the fact that neither here nor now, neither I nor the living world around me, can be isolated in time or space. We are all a part of some infinite, mysterious system, something that adds up to order even if I am not certain of purpose beyond life itself.

There is an old country saying, so true that it is trite, that a late spring means a busy May. This year it was as obvious as the nose on a man's face. Early May was cold and cheerless, but once it warmed up there was so much going on that nobody could really keep up with it. All of spring's unfinished business had to be attended to before June arrived. The truly remarkable fact was that it was all achieved and not one step was skipped.

Hepaticas bloomed, then bloodroot and anemones, then violets and columbines, and only then came apple blossoms and lilacs. Red-winged blackbirds and robins arrived, then flickers and thrashers, then swallows, and the first wave of warblers. Shadblow and swamp maples came to blossom, then poplars and sugar maples; and after the blossoms came the leaves, pastel-pale and even pink and yellow when they first appeared, then all degrees of green as they spread and were suffused with chlorophyll and got down to work. Oats were planted, then corn, and then the kitchen garden. And by June the hayfields were glistening in the sun, rippling in the breeze, green abundance ready for the first cutting. Then the haymakers went to work.

That was the sequence, old as time, old as growth itself. There weren't any loose ends. I am not sure about the easy solutions because I don't know what are the problems, but apparently they are human problems. And when it comes to those, I doubt that there ever were easy solutions. Among the oldest folk tales we know are stories of conflict over thine and mine, and the oldest codes of which we have record consist of thou-shalt-nots. Adam was a rebel, and he had to solve his problems by sweating it out, making his peace with the soil. Whether Adam's story is history or fable doesn't much matter; in it are countless generations of experience that add up to practical truth.

Man can get himself thoroughly snarled up, of course, right in the midst of the land's inexorable order and seasonal insistence. Just a few miles down my valley there was a man who got hopelessly lost in time some years ago. How it began, I don't know, but five years ago I noticed that he was two weeks behind the season. He didn't start his spring plowing until May, didn't get his corn planted till the first week in June, and didn't start cutting hay until July, when the grass was all headed out. The next year he fell behind by another week, and an early fall frost cut his corn crop by half. Two years ago he was planting corn on the Fourth of July, when everybody else's corn was knee-high.

This spring looked like his chance to catch up, but he went to the hospital for a minor operation in the middle of April. I asked why, since he knew he had to have the operation, he didn't go in February. "I didn't have time," he said. Then he added, with a rueful smile, "I can't seem to catch up."

"With this late start," I suggested, "why don't you take this year off and start fresh next spring?"

But he shook his head. "I haven't got time to take the year off. Anyway, the way I'm going it looks like the season's going to catch up with *me* in another year or so."

Life is complex. No one knows that better than the countryman, who lives in the midst of it. But life itself is no more complex than it ever was, really. The problems that won't wrap up in neat, tidy packages arise not from life but from the way we have complicated living, the routines of our days and weeks. Meanwhile, we have the problems of everyone else shouted at us day after day. We aren't merely allowed to participate; we are practically ordered to. In my boyhood we got the world's news, good and bad, once a week and had six days to digest and assort it before the next consignment arrived. Then we began getting it every day and had only twenty-four hours to assimilate it and assess its importance. Now we get it every hour on the hour, fresh, hot, undigested. No wonder we can't find easy solutions. We can't even decide which ones to solve and which ones will solve themselves before sunrise tomorrow. We have pretty well lost our perspective.

If I were eighteen or twenty years old, growing up in a crowd, yammered at day and night by broadcasters telling me what a disordered world this is, I probably would want to turn my back on it too. I might welcome alienation and decide that my own frustrations were the only reality. Instead, I am a man well along in his middle years who, simply by living on the land and apart from the crowds, has become one of a dissenting minority. It is a rather strange feeling to be a radical, at least in the root sense, by holding to fundamentals. I feel engaged with fundamental matters, not alienated. I have no choice—I am a part of them, simply by being a part of life. I have to believe in life, not in its romance but its reality. I must believe in the past, as I am aware of the here and now, just as I believe in the seed and the root, being aware of growth and maturity.

As a dissenter, then, as a countryman forever aware of the land and the environment that fostered my own kind and still tolerates us, I must insist that change is not necessarily chaos and that proliferation is not confusion. Every day of my life I see the proof. Whether my individual life is important or not is pretty much up to me, in the long run. Meanwhile, I do live, and I know sunrise and moonlight, starglow and dawn. I watch flowing water and falling rain, and I am in the midst of such life as growing grass and trees and nesting birds and burrowing beasts, winged insects and crawling worms. I marvel at the seasons and I wonder at the hatching of an egg, whether it be the egg of a mantis or a spider or a domestic hen or a human ovum.

I have just experienced another spring, and I am entering another summer; and unless the averages and the clinical judgment of my doctor are wrong I shall know the exaltation of autumn and the cold beauty of winter and participate in still other springs. That is the way the countryman's life is summarized, by the seasons, not by fretful days and restless nights. The pulse in my wrist is not my pulse alone, separate and apart, but somehow and quite mysteriously a part of the rhythms that beat through the earth and, very likely, the universe. I am a part of the whole. I couldn't alienate myself if I tried.

Meanwhile, we have been cutting hay. That is a part of the season. It happens to be hard, sweaty work; but that, too, is a part of the season, the work. Being here, we work with the land, co-operate. But it is even more than that. The origins of the word "work" reach back to words which meant rites, rituals. In a sense, we are performing a rite, for we are participating in something far greater than ourselves. We are a part of the season, a part of time itself. Maybe there are no ultimate answers, but I will rest on that.

1967—AUTUMN

The Remembering

AFTER the summer's turmoil it was a relief to have the autumn equinox occur not only on schedule but without threats or defiances and with no disturbance whatever. We even had the benevolence of the Harvest Moon, which came to full so close to the equinox that it still lit the sky soon after dusk had dimmed to darkness. No matter what mischief man had been up to, the rhythms by which life abides here on earth were constant and predictable, ticking off time as they have since the oldest rocks were ooze and the first flecks of life were an equivocal phenomenon. There was certainty in the spinning earth and its orbit around the sun, and that certainty made some form of perpetuating life possible and probably inevitable, no matter what upstart man may do to himself.

We hill country people live by that certainty of the earth and its seasons, as do all who live close to the land. It is all around us and quite apart from the hot-handed maneuverings of man. It is in the bud, the leaf, the blossom, the seed. It is in the egg, the chick, the crawling worm, the midge, the moth, and the cawing crow. It is in the lushness of pasture grass and hayfield, in the ripening ear and the bearded head, of corn and oats and wheat and even the wild needle grass. It is as simple as sap-rise in March and as complex as the chatter of wild geese high overhead and arrowing south in November.

Of all the seasons, autumn offers the most to man and requires the least of him. He can plant in the spring, he can till in the summer; but the fact of ripeness is something in which he has no hand whatever. The bounty is there, the ripeness and the maturity, his for the harvesting. The whole spectacle of autumn is there, his for the seeing and understanding. He can harvest or not, as he chooses, and he can see or not, understand or ignore. Unless he holes himself away, deliberately, he will participate to some degree, since autumn doesn't pause at municipal boundaries. But he will become a part of autumn only as he achieves some degree of ripeness and maturity himself, and as he remembers.

Autumn is itself a kind of remembering, a recapitulation, but wholly apart from the doings of man. It generates itself and it sets its own schedules. I could stand under my sugar maples and shout myself hoarse ordering them to turn yellow, as they did a year ago; but until the sun reaches a certain point in its southing and the air cools to a precise degree, nothing would happen. Then, at the time dictated by this particular autumn, those maples turn to shimmering gold without so much as a whisper from anyone of my kind. To be truthful, I never actually tried standing under them and shouting; but I know it would do no good. That is a part of the certainty. The best I could do would be to go out every day and shout, and eventually they would turn and I could say I talked them into it. But that is nonsense. It would put me in the same class with Old Rock.

Old Rock was a coon hound, a beautiful dog with a marvelous voice. He belonged to Jim Nowell, who lived just over the mountain from me. The first year we lived here Old Rock began barking coon in September and kept it up well into November, always at the same clump of poplars high on the mountain. Finally I asked Jim how many coons he had taken out of that place. Jim hesitated, grinned apologetically, and said, "One. I got one coon out of those popples a year ago last week."

"What happens to all the rest of those coons he trees?" I asked.

"He only treed that one," Jim said. "Ever since, he's been barking up that same tree, just hoping there's another coon up there. Old Rock is pretty stupid. But he's got a wonderful voice, hasn't he?"

So far as I know, Old Rock never treed another coon, there or anywhere else. That winter a rabbit hunter from down near Bridgeport, according to the license on his car, stole him, got him into his car and drove away, and Rock never came back. Jim saw it happen and never lifted a finger. He didn't exactly say good riddance, but he did say, "Now maybe I can get my night's sleep and catch up with the chores. It's a relief, not having to go out every night and see if he's finally got another coon treed."

That's one reason I don't holler at the maple trees. I let them color in their own time, knowing that the one at the end of the big barn, which was just a sapling when we came here and now is higher than the barn and the most beautifully symmetrical maple I ever saw, will turn pink and gold ten days after the big maples in front of the house turn yellow. And, like Jim Nowell, I have time to catch up with the chores. See that the roofs are sound on the outbuildings, that the doors don't sag and there are no broken panes in the windows. Bring in the late garden-get and see that it is properly stowed. Make sure there is enough firewood in the woodshed. Check the springhouse, make sure the porcupines haven't gnawed the door off its hinges, as they did one year, or ripped half the paper off the roof. Turn the compost and make new mulch piles of the leaves from the lawn.

And do a bit of remembering. The remembering is one of the seasonal necessities, particularly in the country, and particularly now.

I start remembering when I am doing those seasonal chores. They really don't amount to much, compared to what had to be done right here on this farm fifty or sixty years ago. The evidence is all around me and in the records I can read.

This never was a really isolated farm. Even by road it never was more than five miles from the village, and less than half that if one cut across-lots on foot. But it was a largely self-sufficient establishment for years. It had various cash crops, none of great consequence in total income but all requiring hand labor. But basically it was set up to sustain those who lived here. That was the first purpose, and it was a key to the kind of people who lived here and to the basic attitudes their kind had.

Autumn meant harvest. Not the whole harvest, for a good deal of the harvesting was done throughout the summer, but the last big reaping and storing. There were the certainties of the season, even as now, and unless the folk who lived here abided by them they were courting trouble. The government hadn't yet begun to look after them, nor had the state, and there was a limit to what the neighbors could do, willing as they were, in emergencies. So they made the most of what they had.

On this particular farm the cash crops included milk, tobacco, fruit, butter, eggs, an occasional calf or steer, sawlogs and, in good years, hay and oats, or at least oat straw. Tobacco was an all-summer job, I am sure. It hasn't been grown here in many years, but there once was a tobacco barn beyond the big old cow barn that still stands. The fruit came from a big orchard, apples, pears, peaches and probably cherries, that grew in what is now the home pasture; and there was also a big berry patch, raspberry and blackberry bushes and strawberry beds. Fruit is also an all-summer job, tending, picking, marketing. And the excess couldn't be let go to waste. It was canned or jammed or jellied, or it was made into cider and wine and vinegar. Cows have to be tended to day after day, and so do chickens and ducks and geese, all of which were in the flocks here. Sawlogs are a winter crop, but oats are harvested early and hay is cut in June, again in July and, if the season favors, again in August.

Then came September, autumn, October. The pantries were full. The late garden harvest—potatoes, carrots, beets, squash—were dug and picked, stowed in the cold cellar. Late apples were gathered, the cider press set up, the kegs and barrels readied. Grapes were picked and pressed. The big kettle for apple butter was scrubbed, its chain and tall tripod put in place, with firewood handy.

While these dooryard chores were under way, corn was waiting in the field, ready to be cut or husked. That to be husked in the row was left for later, but that to be cut for fodder was brought into the feed yard and the ears husked out there and stowed in the corn house. And from that feed-yard corn the womenfolk gathered the soft inner husks to stuff ticks for mattresses. I don't know how long the old cornhusk mattresses persisted, but some of them were still around, I am sure, fifty years ago. And feather beds. Another woman-chore was renewing the feather beds and pillows. The plucking of the geese was done before the autumn moult, for the geese were plucked live. Actually, the pluckers took only the loose feathers that were about to be shed.

Then, as soon as hard frost whitened the mornings, came butchering. I failed to mention hogs among the farm's livestock, but they were inevitable. The swillbarrel, and the pigpen constituted the farmer's highly efficient garbage disposal unit; and when the hogs had been properly fattened on a supplement of corn they provided the ham and bacon, the sausage and side meat, to go with eggs and sauerkraut and beans and potatoes. So the butchering was done, in clouds of steam and smoke; the lard was tried out, the sausage was made, the meat was salted and pickled and hung in the smokehouse where hickory smouldered for days. And a little later, when the cold had really settled in, a young steer was butchered, too, for steaks and roasts and soup meat and hamburger and corned brisket. Some years, when the calves all ran to heifers, the farmer and his son went up on the mountain and brought back a couple of fat young bucks, and venison took the place of beef.

There were a few sheep, but there wasn't much spinning done here fifty years ago, and no weaving, I am sure. The grannies probably spun yarn now and then, from special wool they had saved out when the sheep were shorn and the wool marketed; but they made yarn for their knitting. And by then flax was just a pretty blue flower in the garden. Nobody retted flax or spun linen threat at home. But you can be sure the women went to the village on bright autumn days, while the road was still in good condition, and traded eggs and butter for bolt-cloth, yards and yards of it, to make up into dresses and shirts during the winter.

And for the youngsters there was school, at the Weatogue School a mile and a half down the road. It still stands, now made over completely, the residence, fittingly, of a schoolmaster, the head of one of our regional state colleges, who drives thirty miles to his office every day. There was school, with chores to be done before they went and after they got home, barn chores, yard chores, house chores for every youngster beyond the toddler stage.

Remembering all this now, this quiet rural autumn morning, I wonder what we have gained and what we have lost as we, a nation, have become so largely an urban people, not only living apart from the land but alien to it. We haven't achieved certainty, about ourselves or even about our purposes. Man has become one of the most unpredictable creatures on earth, and for that reason one of the least reliable. Biologically, he came late on the scene, and now he has achieved the means of removing himself early; it is now a matter of choice what he will do with that means, and man has steadily diminished both the area of choice and the willingness to choose. Lacking the continuity of the seasons and the certainty of the great rhythms inescapable on the land, he has achieved a strange arrogance that mistakes data for knowledge and makes gods of his machines.

Nobody in his right mind would argue that isolated life on the land, wholly dependent on the seasons and made comfortable only by individual effort, represented the ultimate of human achievement. But it is debatable whether automated, group-dominated urban life, almost wholly isolated from the natural environment, represents that ultimate either. Civilization and culture should include respect for the individual and some understanding of the world around you. There is something basically wrong with any culture that submerges the individual, exalts the machine, and deliberately isolates itself from the land, no matter how many automobiles, color television sets, and electric toothbrushes it may make each year. There was a time and there was a way of life in which we had other purposes and other gauges of achievement.

Maybe I shouldn't be remembering. Maybe I should be examining the present. But this is not nostalgia. The past, too, had its evils. This really is the aftermath of turmoil and violence in the dark canyons and infested caves of the human condition today. It is a look back at who we were and where we came from, trying to find recognizable faces in the frenzied crowd shouting, "Kill! Burn!" It is saying that we once knew certainty, lived with it and by it, and that we moved away and forgot.

1967—WINTER

Down to Earth

I DON'T RECALL a better example of how literally down-to-earth are the seasons than we have had the past few months. There were days when I wondered if the seasons themselves weren't in revolt against the technicians, who so often think that measurements and data add up to omniscience if not actual omnipotence. By astral computations, the seasons are almost as firmly established as Euclid's axioms; but where people live the seasons are a matter of weather, the day-to-day changes that originate right here on earth. Not one year in twenty does spring begin with the vernal equinox or winter with the winter solstice.

This year, here in the New England hills, autumn came on the very first day of September, not on the twenty-third as the computation had ordained. There wasn't any question about it. August ended, summer moved out overnight, and here was autumn. All in all, September was a splendid autumn month, brightened by a brilliant Harvest Moon at the proper time but indulging in no equinoctial tantrums. It simply ignored the equinox. In fact, the only out of the ordinary happening, and it didn't really break the autumn calm, was the brief visit by the hippies.

Where they came from, I still don't know, but one perfect day in mid-month six young barefoot outlanders appeared. The first I knew of them was when I saw them on my way to the village. They were tenderfooting it along the gravelly, thorny shoulder of our back road. All had long hair, three had beards, and two quite obviously were girls. They had wilted asters in their hair and they stopped from time to time to pull stickers from their feet and stare ecstatically at the roadside meadows and wooded hills.

I drew up beside these young pilgrims in ragged jeans and asked if I could be of help, if perhaps they were lost, since they were several miles from the main highway. One of the bearded young men smiled at me and said, "Lost? Man, *you're* the one who's lost! We are found, at last." And one of the young females tossed a wilted calico aster into my lap and intoned a benediction: "Peace. Love."

When I came back from Canaan an hour later they had vanished. I don't know how long they continued "found" in our beautiful autumn valley, but late the next day a filling station man over on the main road said "six bare-footed bums," as he called them, passed his place just after noon, walking south and trying to thumb rides.

It was too bad they didn't stay longer. September, as I was saying, was a beautiful fall month, end to end, and October was comfortable as well as colorful beyond any but the most hackneyed superlatives. Maybe they will remember the serenity of this land when it is so full of asters that they overflow the roadsides, white and lavender and purple; but I rather wish they had seen it in full October color. It was a sight that made the psychedelic fantasy-art that I have seen look like kindergarten experiments with watercolor paint. And the only trip you had to take to see it was out into the dooryard or up or down the road.

But it's just as well they didn't linger on into November. Autumn ended this year with October, six weeks ahead of the winter soltice. November was winter, just like that. The temperature skidded into the teens and low twenties, crept warily up toward forty at midday, then cowered back into the twenties night after night. And that was the end of the flowers. It snowed. Ponds iced over. There was frost in the ground. And we natives, who also believe in love and peace and like to sit and listen to the bees, had to snug the house and barn and do the December chores a month early. We learned quite a while back that without four walls, a roof, a fire, and something in the pantry, we have trouble lasting through till the first violets bloom again.

I heard some people suggest that the year was out of kilter, that time had got all twisted. One man who specializes in letters to the editor wrote indignantly that the air pollution was to blame, that if we didn't do something about power plants and automobiles and incinerators we would bring on a new ice age by 1970. Another man blamed it all on the sun spots. Still another said it was a result of all this orbiting and rocketing, which had upset the natural balances and interrupted the solar currents and the atmospheric plasma, whatever that is.

But it wasn't really that time was out of joint, as Mr. Shakespeare's moody Dane said it some years ago. It was that we were caught off guard by those crashing atmospheric tides that always send winter surging down the latitudes like a seventh wave on an open beach. We hadn't expected early winter, but here it was. Thank goodness, though, it wasn't another situation we had to set right, or even try to. The seasons never are right or wrong. They may be early or late, according to our expectations, but basically they simply *are,* like a great many other things. If we would only refrain from moralizing and trying to impose rules where they don't apply, we would have a lot more time to enjoy life. For love, let's say, and for peace.

Maybe the mice haven't any bearing on these matters, but I am sure they have some significance, perhaps even a profound one. If I had time I might even fashion some kind of fable about the mice. Instead, I shall only tell what happened.

A few miles from my farmhouse is a large estate belonging to a man of comfortable means and with a sense of the fitness of things. When he built the big house he specified that the electric power line must be brought in underground so there would be no disfiguring overhead wires. So the cables were brought in to a concrete pit, a kind of manhole, where the big transformer was installed, and from there the feeder lines fanned out to the various buildings.

The first week in November when winter, as I said, really got a firm hold on this area, the local power company's emergency service office received a telephone call from the caretaker at this estate at 3:15 one morning. The power was off, he said. His electric blanket went dead, the cold wakened him, he found that the lights wouldn't work, and the furnace had quit. The man at emergency service said he would send someone right out. Then he summoned the repairman who was on call that night and told him to go out there and find the mouse. The repairman said, "It can't be the mouse. It's only November." But he went, he found the mouse and he came back and reported the service restored, everything back to normal.

What happened was simple. The transformer pit is supposed to be sealed shut, impervious to intruders. But the transformer generates a certain amount of heat and every winter a field mouse, looking for a warm place as soon as the temperature gets down to the twenty-degree mark, somehow manages to get into the pit. Once in there, that mouse isn't content to settle down and enjoy the warmth. It has to poke and explore, maybe gathering mouse-data for some mouse-purpose. Before long it stands on one side of the main switch, sniffs the other side and, *puff!* A fuse blows. The lines go dead, and so does the mouse.

The power people expect this to happen about the third week in December. But a mouse, not knowing much about degree-days or the winter solstice, gets into the transformer pit when the tip of its tail says it's time to find a warm place to sleep. No mouse, of course, ever returns to tell the other mice what's in the pit, so it may be that the whole mouse tribe thinks, if it thinks at all, that the pit is some kind of mouse heaven. Or hell, maybe. Silly wondering.

I heard about another mouse from the furnace serviceman who came to find what caused an alarming thump in the blower in our furnace. "I hope," he said as he started down to the basement, "it isn't a mouse." He found the trouble within five minutes, put on a new drive belt, and it was fixed. Very simple. Then I asked him about the mouse.

He had just come from a service call down the road a mile or so, a thump or knock in a furnace. And he found a mouse caught in the "squirrel cage," as they call the drum-type fan used in many systems to blow warm air from the furnace through the ducts into the house. "It got into the system," he said, "maybe through a duct, and followed it down to the blower, which probably wasn't running at the time. Then the furnace and the blower went on, and there was the mouse, caught. It had to run like a squirrel in one of those wheels in a cage. Finally it got tired out and tried to escape between two vanes in the fan, and it got stuck. A couple of times around and the banging killed it. And there it was, going bump, bump, bump every time the blower went on." He frowned and asked "What do you suppose a mouse thinks about in a spot like that?"

I didn't guess then and I won't guess now. All I know is that the mouse in the blower, like the mouse in the transformer pit, didn't know or care whether it was April or November. All it knew was that the tip of its tail got cold and it had to do something about it. It got caught in what has to be called a mouse-race, and there wasn't any way out. And statistics, data, calculations of the solstices and equinoxes, made not one whit of difference. Just as the statistics and the averages didn't change the weather.

Right now I am sitting here in my study, looking out the side window, watching it snow. The snow comes down gently, without a breath of wind. It sifts through the big apple tree in the back yard, the flakes idling down and disappearing on the snow-covered grass. If I opened the window and listened closely I might hear the faint sound of those flakes nudging each other as they fall, it is so quiet. A little while ago there was a flock of juncos under the tree, feeding on millet spilled from the feeders we hang there. The tree sparrows get into the feeders and kick out the grain, scratching automatically. But something, maybe a shadow that vaguely resembled a hawk or an owl, alarmed the juncos and they rose in a flittering flock and scattered.

Beyond the apple tree and the back yard is the home pasture, now covered with snow, and beyond the pasture is Tom's Mountain. There is just enough snow falling to make the mountain misty and mysterious. I can barely make out the contours of its crest. It is mysterious, the way all mountains are, because something made the earth's crust wrinkle, long ago, and the wrinkles became the mountains. We know how old are the mountains' rocks, and whether they were formed hot or cold, and we can analyze them right down to the ultimate atoms. But we don't know whether the earth shrank or expanded or contorted in some kind of vast, cosmic frown. All we know is that there were wrinkles, and more winters than we can count gnawed at those wrinkles, and finally a series of ice ages sliced off most of the highlands, ripped out brand new valleys, and changed everything again. What caused the ice ages? There is quite an assortment of answers, all the way from a shifting axis to dust in the atmosphere. Which would you prefer?

I was out the other afternoon doing the outdoor chores that must be done, even in winter, if you live in the country. Out by the barn, which now is only a storage place, no longer a cow barn, a cottontail rabbit suddenly took flight, almost literally. It bounded out of the snow and went through the barnyard and across the back lot to the brushy fencerow in a crystal cloud. It was running for its life, as a rabbit always does when it runs. And I wondered what a rabbit thinks of an early winter. Or a raccoon. Or a fox. Or a woodchuck.

Silly wondering again. What any of them thinks, if anything, can't change the weather one whit, for them or for us. But at least they don't fight back. Could it be that they, too, only want to live and listen to the bees buzzing among the flowers?

I came back to the house thinking that at least I know the year complete, snowflakes as well as daisies. I don't really resent the necessity of a coat and a roof; I appreciate the comfort they provide. My kind may go scribble, scribble, scribble, gathering the data, the averages, the norms, the percentages, and pluses and minuses. They may feed it into the computers and decode the answers. What they come out with, actually, is pretty much what we knew before they put the question: "When autumn ends early, winter comes early." Which is not too bad a finding, at that. It is almost as profound as saying that today is bounded by yesterday and tomorrow.

So that's where we come out. And I am satisfied, because I didn't have to wait for a message from the tip of a tail I discarded far away and long ago, back along the path up from the steamy swamps and soupy seas where life began—we think.

1968—SPRING

April and Integrity

BEING rather well acquainted with woodchucks and weather, we have a slight variation on the Groundhog Day legend. (A groundhog, of course, is only a woodchuck with a publicity agent.) Up here in the hills we hope the groundhog will see his shadow and assure us of *only* six more weeks of winter. Actually, the earliest I ever saw a woodchuck out of his den was March 10. And if winter really lets go its grip by the first of April we call it an early spring. We sometimes get snow in May here in the Connecticut hills.

We always hope, then, for a sunny Groundhog Day and an early spring because they will involve us again in constructive fundamental matters, and maybe even will get our perspective back in working order. Winter is an introspective time at best, a season in which the ordinary follies of mankind become a burden on the conscience. Away, way back, February was a purification ceremony, remember. But this year the madness of mankind, combined with the load of guilt we have been told is ours to carry until the end of time, was almost overwhelming.

We welcomed the weather we got at the turn of the year—a foot and a half of snow and temperatures down to fifteen and twenty below with several days in a row when the high was less than five above zero. That kind of weather is almost as good as an early spring to keep a man busy and divert his mind from mischief. So we shoveled snow, pitched hay and manure, cut wood, built up the fires, and waited for the January thaw to bring a breather.

The thaw came, just about on schedule, though in an ordinary year we wouldn't have called it more than a break in the weather. The temperature got up to thirty and stayed there several days, dropping only into the low twenties at night. Compared to the lows of only a week earlier, the temperature had risen fifty degrees, and that's a thaw in our language. By Groundhog Day there was enough sun to cast a visible shadow. But by then the affairs of man were in such a state that we didn't pay much attention to mythical portents. There were so many real portents that we sort of let the seasons take care of themselves for a while.

I note this because it is so unusual. Here in the valley we usually take it upon ourselves to tally the storms, measure the snowdrifts, watch the barometer, keep track of the temperature, see that the moon's phases are in order, and generally supervise such matters. It is the tradition that somebody has to do this, and with such a relative few of us left on the land we have a double responsibility.

But this year we let things go for two or three weeks while we were preoccupied with guilt and worry about the state of the dollar, the plight of the cities, and the realities of politics, taxes, and war. We worried right through Lincoln's birthday and Valentine's Day and Washington's birthday. The next day was Friday, the moon was in its last quarter, daylight had increased more than three-quarters of an hour since Groundhog Day. It was high time to get back to fundamentals.

We got back, and found that we hadn't even been missed. It was quite obvious that everything was in order, right down to the quickening of the color in the red osier dogwood stems. When I checked the calendar I found that it was only four weeks until the vernal equinox. Everything that mattered, from a root in the ground to the orbit of the earth around the sun, was exactly as the big schedule of life and time required. And there it was again, staring me in the face, that same old lesson that man never seems to learn: Man is dispensable; the earth doesn't need him.

Not wanting to carry the message any further at that moment, I got back to work at those pretentious chores that proclaim my tenancy here. A man has to appear needed and busy at important tasks, no matter what he may be thinking when he lies awake at two A.M. I began cleaning up the winter's trash under the big weeping willow out by the old milk house we use as a garage. I pruned the grape vines. I cut a clump of sumac that threatened to take a grassy bank along the river in front of the house. I went up on the mountain and cleaned out the springhouse that provides our water a good part of the year.

It was all good exercise, and it accomplished things

that had to be done if we are to continue to live here in comfort and satisfaction. But time after time I found myself wondering why I was doing those things instead of cutting trees, rooting out vines, dumping my trash and garbage on the riverbank and in the river, fouling springs and using brooks as sewers. That way I would be asserting my dominance over the environment, wouldn't I? I would be showing somebody, or something, how all-powerful I am.

The answer, of course, was as plain as the prominent nose on my own face. I, individually, didn't have to show anybody how all-powerful I am—*if* I am. The competition by which we live most of the time may be between man and man, but the conditions of our continued existence are between man and earth, his environment. Somewhere along the line someone is going to have to stop tearing things apart, society as well as the physical world, and accept the fundamental truth that man's tenure here is a consequence of biologically fortuitous coincidence, as nearly as we can trace it, and could be terminated as easily as was that of the dinosaurs. The giant reptiles, according to an eminent geneticist and a well-known astrophysicist, may have been wiped out by massive doses of radiation from the nearby explosion of bright stars. There have been 182 supernova explosions, they calculate, which could have killed or greatly altered animal life on earth, possibly even created the human race as a biological sport.

Anyway, there was my answer, and I didn't even feel guilty about it. If one starts accepting guilt for today's cult of violence, say, one must go on from there and accept guilt for the ritual killing of the virgins by the Aztecs, or for the vengeance murders in ancient Greece. If one must bear the load of guilt for the whole human race, we have been a damned species from the time of Cain.

And with that answer I slept somewhat better, though the dawn was coming at around five-thirty by then, the migrant birds were arriving by the flock, and the early mornings echoed with vernal music. I won't even try to explain, but I have found the songs of birds most distracting when I am trying to worry, so I give it up at least until the birds settle down a bit, get over their first frenzy of song, which seems to be a kind of homecoming celebration that lasts about three weeks. Incidentally, I have wondered if the early chorus of bird song is so annoying to many urban visitors to the country simply because it interrupts their worrying. They say it interrupts their sleep, I know; but even their sleep seems to be pretty restless.

Where we go from here, of course, is anybody's guess, and it has seemed, the past few weeks, as though there was a great deal of guesswork going on in places where there might better have been substantial tallying up of facts. We are fortunate—and the "we" does not include humanity as a whole; we who live close to the land are fortunate, as I was saying, in being in the midst of truth. The truth of a pasture, for example, where the grass will grow from its roots if we give it half a chance and keep our hot hands under control. The truth of a woodland, where the trees can't falsify a leaf or a nut or a key, and set down the record of each year, indelible and exactly as it is, in the rings about its bole. The truth of a brook, water that flows downhill, that is sweet to begin with and will keep itself clean if it has half a chance. The truth of the air and the sky and the sunrise, of the rain, the dew, the thunderstorm.

What is truth? That old question has had so many expedient answers that you have to be careful where you ask it. When I ask it here at the foot of the mountain the answer is that truth is the way things are, not the way we shape them or contrive them or wish they were, but the way they are. So our lives, at least here on the land, are bounded by truth, the truthful elements. What we make of those lives is another matter, and I would rather not go into it too deeply just when April is near at hand. April, of all times, is the very epitome of integrity, of truth in action and in being. It is rather difficult to live with April, where April has a chance, and not somewhat partake of the season's elements.

Put it this way: April is the end of March and February, with January still further back and out of the picture. April is what we think of when we are full of idealism and hope—April as a month, that is, as a season in the sun and on the earth. April is what the best dreams and the highest motives might make of life, for it is spring and beginnings. It is pussy willows turning golden with the pollen of fertility. It is the hylas calling frantically for mates and all their tribe laying eggs in the chill waters of the swamps. It is hepaticas in bloom and violets in bud and the youngest of tender young leaflets showing tips in the unberbrush of the woodland. It is swamp maples in bloom. It is grass green, young, tender, reaching out to cover the whole of this scarred, battered earth with healing green. It is melt and ooze and flow, the sweet runoff of this earth's innocent waters from the uplands where trees still grow, rocks still are mossy, the land is still clean.

April is young, innocent only in the sense that it has committed no crime, and full of the year's wisdom. April has no sense of guilt, though it may have sprung from a brutal January, a February that starved bird and froze beast, and a March that flooded many an inhabited valley. April is now on the threshold, and the genesis of tomorrow, which may or may not be a better tomorrow but certainly will have all the mating and rooting and sprouting and greening that belong to the season. April is what it is, and no pretense about it. It is sex without a snicker or a leer. It is every kind of mating there is, animal and plant, and no prurience. It is birth. It is, as I was saying, spring and beginnings. And if we would only look for truth rather than for visions, for reality rather than abstractions, there it is, waiting.

But—and this may be the very nub of the matter—April, spring, change, new beginnings, the whole of it and immeasurably more, would go on and on without any watching from us. It doesn't await our discovery. There really isn't time for that, in the big scheme. April, or spring, or any season, cannot wait for man to make peace with himself and forget his absurd dreams of universal mastery, his swaggering pose of omnipotence. They cannot wait, and they will not wait. We find them or we don't, and that's the whole of it. We know or we go on being arrogantly ignorant in our scientific, machine-fed, computer-dictated race to oblivion.

Or perhaps we become acquainted with woodchucks and weather and try to live with the world and ourselves. We reject the demand that we chant "*Mea culpa*" morning, noon, and night. We reject the circumstantial lie and the expedient half-truth, prefering the acid-bite and even the gut-agony of truth itself. And we despise the liars. We reject the crowd, which too often is a headless, mindless, merciless beast. We are even skeptical of the System, which turns its back on all the Aprils of the race and the world and tries to wall us off in a timeless, airless, sunless, megalopolitan synthesis dictated by the computers to fulfill our unrealized potentialities.

We reject them, and we laugh at woodchuck shadows and make our own variations on the legends. But we do remember the legends. We remember when everyone knew April. We remember when there were dreams, not nightmares. Remembering, we look forward to April again. We expect to awaken to bird song in April. Early spring or late, we are still a part of it. Each spring, we ask no more than that, expect no more. Without belief, what is there left?

The Flow of Time

YEAR AFTER YEAR July seems to creep up behind us, and, since "Bang!" now is outlawed virtually everywhere, shout "Boo!" to remind us that the year is half finished. We did note the summer solstice ten days ago, but even that seemed out of place and ahead of time. It was only a couple of weeks ago, or so it seemed, that we were in the midst of the warmest April on record here in our hill country, planting peas and onion sets and lettuce and carrots, and having to remind ourselves that it isn't safe to put out tomato plants till the end of May. And here we are now, picking fresh peas, living high on green beans and baby beets and carrots and such lettuce as you never can get in the market, and drooling over tomatoes big as golf balls and green as grass, wondering whether they will ripen before the corn is ready, hoping the raccoons don't find the corn before we get a chance at it.

Yesterday it was April. Today it is July.

Time is out of joint. Not only the times, but time, that *tempus* that even the old Romans knew tends to *fugit.* Ovid said so, and about the same time he was saying that another poet whose full name was Quintus Horatius Flaccus was compressing into one sentence all that I tried to say in a whole paragraph. "Summer," Horace said, "treads on heels of spring."

There may be some comfort in knowing this isn't a new phenomenon, a product of rocketry, radar, laser and the computers, but I don't find it very soothing comfort chiefly because the air echoes with peremptory words, "Hurry, hurry, hurry!" and I don't know whether we are hurrying toward heaven or running madly away from hell. All I know is that when I ask "Why?" there is no audible answer.

But even that is not new either. Last night I was re-reading a book by Brooks Atkinson, "Once Around the Sun," and in a July entry—the year was 1951,—he wrote, of the morning newspaper, "Ah, yes, the news is ominous. Revolution, war, political crises, deficit financing, business recession, threats to civil liberties—the whole structure of the world appears to be collapsing." Obviously, we have been running madly for a long time now, and whether to or from doesn't seem to matter much. So, even up here, away from the crowds, we have to get outdoors and sit down, now and then, and let time flow through us as it does through the universe. We have to listen for another beat, another rhythm.

Back in mid-April, when the affairs of man had reached a dismal summary of madness and murder, followed by arson and pillage, we spent a long evening watching a spectacular full moon climb the sky, slowly go into eclipse, slowly emerge again, and continue its stately journey across the heavens. Quite apart from any meaning the eager symbolist might find, that was an evening when the affairs of men seemed almost picayune and the particular follies of the day made no sense whatever. If all human life were blotted out, that same shadow would have crossed the moon precisely as it did, and the course of the earth, moon and sun would continue totally unchanged.

A little later we spent a late afternoon on the open deck of a boathouse at a nearby lake, facing the whole lake and the tumbled hills beyond to the west. It was an afternoon away from the telephone and casual passers-by, a time alone with the water and the sky and the hills. Shadbush was just opening bud. Hepatica was in bloom, and bloodroot and anemone. There was just enough air in motion to make the water lap at the rocks along the shoreline, that eternal slap of water on stone that has created virtually all the sand on earth, a sound that makes me think of the hourglass of the eons, pebbles grinding into sand which flows forever through the slender neck of time itself.

We sat there on the deck as the sun deliberately eased toward the hilltop horizon, gilding the water and shimmering hosts of newly-hatched gnats, creatures of only a few brief days, like dancing clouds of twinkling silver motes freshly evaporated from the lake itself. High overhead a red-tailed hawk sailed with scarcely a feather's quiver, circling slowly and gradually working its way toward the hills. We watched the hawk until we lost it in the sun, and when I closed my eyes all I could see was the blinding dazzle, a timeless star so bright even my eyelids couldn't shut it out. The afternoon flowed away, the sun settled behind the glowing hills, the lake was a vast shimmer of light reflected from a darkening sky for a long time, and at last there was darkness and there were stars overhead and stars in the still-lapping water, stars that rocked and danced while the water ground a few more grains of sand.

In May I went out along the riverbank and watched the opening of buds on the sugar maples, deliberate as the emergence of stars in the night sky. I saw the way the giant mullein stalk begins to climb from the gray-green rosette of winter leaves, a six-foot stalk that would take three months to grow and bloom and make its seeds. I saw the milkweeds come up like asparagus shoots and leaf out and prepare to bloom, blossoms with the scent of honeysuckle and tuberose, which would become silvery-green goosehead pods that would not ripen and burst and strew their airy cargo till October.

Time, the passage of the season, the lunar month, the day. Time hasn't changed a noticeable fraction of a second in ten million years. The first man who stood on his two feet and faced the sunrise and had a glimmering of wonder about time knew no longer span of daylight than I know today. Grass grew as deliberately then as now, and buds opened and the moon had its phases, just as today.

But somewhere along the way man, the incurable counter, was no longer content to number his years and his days. He must number his hours, too. So he invented the clock to divide the days into hours. Then to split the hours into minutes. Into seconds. Microseconds. Faster, faster, fasterfasterfaster. But even the microseconds still add up to the same year the seconds did, and the minutes, the hours, the days. Time itself is unchanged, but man has snared himself in his own time-traps.

As I said, we had an early spring. By late April we told ourselves we were two weeks ahead of normal. Then May came and evened things off, as it always does. By the end of May we were right where we always are, ready to start haying. Oh, maybe we were a few days ahead of ordinary, but not much. We said, and we believed that we were right on schedule. Whether we gain or lose two weeks in March and April doesn't much matter, because we don't gain an hour, really, or lose one, in the long run. It's all a part of the season and the year; it adds up to the same total, time after time. There's so much to be done, and just so much time to do it. Nature somehow apportions the energy to get it done, and when we know what we are doing we do pretty much the same thing.

But last spring, just when we were getting the garden planted and the new alfalfa started in the lower meadow where the weeds had almost taken over, there was a most peculiar report from the West Coast. A group called the Southern California Research Council made a kind of analysis of sociological trends and came up with the same old hackneyed finding that we are going to have more leisure than we know what to do with in the next twenty years, then went on to say that the average American is worried about having too much spare time because of "the so-called work-ethic —the claim that work is good for the soul and stands higher intrinsically on the social scale of values than play or time off." And it said, "We have not yet begun to develop a substitute principle for the sanctity of work." This obviously was the next thing that must be done to save our endangered soul and our social scale of values.

That, as I say, was just when April was pushing into May and things were getting ready for June; and as I read that report I wondered just what kind of never-never land these theorists inhabit. How anybody with a grain of sense could recommend a substitute for the idea of work in the spring is beyond me. Maybe in late July or August, or maybe between New Year's and Groundhog Day, but not in April or May when every natural force in sight is working around the clock, getting things going. I don't know how it is in California —I haven't been there in some years—but I know that if I were to sit down out in the side yard here and try to develop a leisure-ethic, even at the end of June, I would soon be grown over by grass and weeds and it wouldn't be long before my bones would be bleaching.

I can't imagine where those sociologists got the notion that the work-ethic is passé. Without it there would be no income; with no income there would be no taxes; without taxes there would be nothing for the government to appropriate as subsidies and to sustain those industries that provide most of the spending money in Southern California and Texas. Without work-ethic income we would, perforce, have a leisure-ethic bigger than we had back in the early 1930s. I hope that isn't what they are advocating.

It may be that, since Southern Califonia is well stocked with retired people living on pensions, annuities and Social Security, the researchers think all people, of all ages, can and should live on the same basis. If so, I have a little secret to share with them. Annuities, pensions and Social Security all are based on the negotiable products of the work-ethic—income, investments, and taxes. If there is some other way to finance them, word of it hasn't got to this part of the country yet. I shan't lie awake nights waiting to hear it, I might add.

Mind you, I am not even hinting that there's anything sacred about work. But it isn't a curse, either. Everywhere I look I see that living things work and only dead and dying things don't work. Even those lilies of the field which, according to the Scriptures, neither toil nor spin, do work. The roots gather food from the soil, the leaves create sugars and starches by photosynthesis, and the blossoms create seeds for perpetuation of the species. Every plant, every bird, every animal, every insect expends energy in the process of sustaining life and achieving growth. They work. If they didn't, there would be very little difference between January and July except in the temperature of the air. But in that case, there wouldn't be anybody here to know or to discuss the merits of work and leisure.

We are so reluctant to learn, or even to acknowledge the obvious truths all around us. We keep trying to get away from the natural world, or to change it into something different. We keep talking about "our world," instead of recognizing that we are only squatters here, tenants who happen to be tolerated. We didn't create anything here but the cities and their appurtenances, and in the end they are dependent on the country. Isolate a city for thirty days and that city suffers and faces ruin and death. Even in the summer time, when the natural world is as nearly hospitable to every form of life as one could wish. Cut off a city's water, its outside sources of food or even its throbbing lines of power from distant sources, and see how many July or August days it can survive. Not even a full-blown leisure-ethic can make such a beleaguered metropolis tolerable.

But that, we hope, is beside the point. With luck, the cities will not be so beleaguered, and we will somehow get through another summer. And we folk up here in the hills will sweat, as usual, through the summer work and have no more than the usual complaints, chiefly because we still recognize the common principle that I suppose must be called the work-ethic, though it really isn't much more than the old truism that a man must earn his way in this world somehow. As I said, we are picking peas now and hoping we get roasting ears before the coons find that they are prime, in another month or so. That's a part of what I mean. We planted those peas and those rows of corn, and we weeded and hoed and tended them. We worked for them.

I admit that there were times, right in the midst of haying or other seasonal work, when I heard that ghostly voice shouting, "Hurry, hurry, hurry!" And I wondered why and for what. Then I looked around and knew that the trees and the grass and even the sun and the moon paid no attention to such orders. And it wasn't hard to settle down and keep to the rhythm of the day and the season. And every now and then, when the outside pressure gets a little too strong, we go down to the lake and watch the stars in the gently lapping water and listen to the grinding of a few more grains of sand. When I listen closely I can hear the soft whisper of sand flowing through the neck of the hourglass, the same flow it has had since time began.

A Song for October

OCTOBER comes and one walks with autumn in the city park, along the suburban street, beside the country road and in every woodland. For October is the time of the falling leaf, the ripened nut, the crispness underfoot. Now we are surrounded by the earthy browns, the vivid yellows and sere tans, by the aster-purples and the sumac-reds, the transformed leftovers of summer shade, bringing the brilliance of autumn down to earth around us.

Out in the dooryard this morning, just looking, feeling, being a part of the new day, I glanced down the river and saw the clump of aspens down at the bend, twinkling in their golden leaf, shimmering in the sunlight. I saw them and I remembered words from an old Navaho prayer song:

Beauty before me, I return.
Beauty above me, I return.
Beauty below me, I return.
Beauty all around me, with it I return.
Now on the trail of beauty, there I return.

The words are from one of the songs of Dawn Boy in the Mountain Chant, and I felt a little like Dawn Boy himself returning with the day, another new day, beauty all around me. Just remembering took me back to the Southwest, where the quaking aspens now are full of shimmering gold and the scrub oak makes the foothills rich with the color of warm red wine. We here in the Northeast have no such song to match our autumn. Perhaps the Mahicans who once lived here in Weatogue did have such songs celebrating the beauty of the oaks and maples and flaming sumacs. If so, we have lost and forgotten them, as we forget so many simple things that have no present monetary value.

The maples do remain, however, and the durable oaks and the short-lived but persistent sumac, and every autumn they remind me of unsung songs I would like to hear. Instead, even here in the distant hills, we hear the deafening clap and feel the shattering impact of sonic booms that make the very earth shudder. That, some of my technician friends tell me, is the song of tomorrow, when super-sonic transports will be tearing the sky to shreds and, the technical fellows insist, "revising our concept of time." They don't seem to realize that they aren't talking about time at all. They are talking about speed. Time can't be changed. There it is, day after day, year after year, just as it was, precisely the same dimensions, when man first achieved the conception of a day and a year.

But I was talking about autumn and songs, not the screams and shattering blasts of super-sonic jets.

There is an old notion that autumn is a melancholy

time best suited to dirges and sad laments. Bryant wrote of its days as "the saddest of the year." But I know of few places on this continent where autumn fails to provide some of the most beautiful days of the year. The dust of summer has begun to settle, first hard frost clears the air, and October skies can be as clear and blue as a baby's eyes. Even Indian Summer, with its haze and its misty dawns, has a special lure. October, in fact, is responsible for Fall fever, the very antithesis of Spring fever. In early May there is a lassitude and a compulsion to lie on your back in the new green grass and let the answers, if there are any of importance, come to you. But in October there is an almost irresistable wanderlust that is the very essence of search and adventure, the need to go and find answers on the far side of the beckoning hills.

October is not really a summation. It is achievement, rather, without finality. Spring was all eagerness and new beginnings. Summer was growth and sweaty industry. June was hay and fireflies. July was hot afternoons and crashing thunderstorms and hay that couldn't be got in earlier because June was too wet. August was corn pollen in the sultry air, the shrilling of the harvest flies, dog days, long restless nights. Summer was both accomplishment and frustration—rain when haymakers needed sun, talk when idle people needed jobs, politics when the times called for statesmanship. But we got through to September and a measure of relief and relaxation, for the countryside at least. September was a month with an early full moon and a new moon for the equinox.

And now nature's urgencies are past. This is a time of ripeness, of wholeness, of plenty. It must have been about now, this time of the year, when Adam ate the forbidden fruit which had ripened to perfection. And it surely was now that one of Adam's sons discovered the potentialities in a ripe grape. The seasons come to fulfillment, not necessarily for the delight and satisfaction of man but in their own ineluctable procession. If he is both wise and fortunate, a man should be able to find some measure of contentment now.

But, as I was just saying, October also brings Fall fever, and a man can't help hearing the high-honking geese. He has to get up and go, if he can wrench a foot loose, just to see what a big, magnificient world this really is before he can come home again and settle down for the winter. I sometimes think of October as a do-as-you-damn-please time of the year, and we could do far worse than set the whole month aside as such a holiday. The only stricture should be that you mustn't please to go tromping on other people's toes. Even that might not be too much of a problem, though, because tempers usually aren't as short in October as they were in July and August. There's usually at least a trace of courtesy in the autumn air.

I don't know quite how you could accommodate the quadrennial spate of bombastic flatulence that marks our presidential campaigns, but maybe we could find a way to rule that out for the duration of October. Declare a political holiday and give us the whole thirty-one days to recover from the bombiliation. Then we could go to the polls the first week in November more or less rested up and in a state of at least theoretical sanity. If anyone fears the consequences of making such short shrift of the political campaign, I suggest that he take a look at the results of the campaigns and presidential elections over the past century. The fact that the republic has survived them proves that it is made of rawhide, whalebone and rock maple.

But since there's not the proverbial snowball's chance of having October declared such a national holiday this year, we have decided to declare our own equivalent. I am hooking a timer to the TV and radio that will cut them off after two minutes, no matter what program is on. We are declaring ourselves not at home to any comers, friends, kinfolk or total strangers. We are, for a while, going to be as free as the October wind. We think we are, anyway, and that's the important thing.

The fall chores are in hand. We have finished canning tomatoes, the only garden product we still preserve that way. We have eaten our season's fill of snap beans, carrots, beets and garden lettuce, and the late endive is trussed and blanching for November, when we will be hungry for greens again. Frost put an end to the fecundity of summer squash; maybe there are those who mourn the demise of zucchini and yellow crookneck after Labor Day, but I am not among them. Tomorrow we will bring in the winter squash, the kind with a green and orange complexion and a Turk's cap on its head, to ripen-off till Thanksgiving. Parsnips and Brussels sprouts need a good, hard frost before they are fit for the table, so they can be let alone for now.

Farm chores are pretty well taken care of by mid-

September, now that most of the field corn goes into the silo. A man doesn't cut fence posts or mend fences except in special instances until next spring, when he is so winter-weary and so tired of being housebound he will do almost anything to get outdoors, even set posts and string barbed wire. I shall give the grass a final mowing in the front yard, so the leaves that come down from the big maples can blow away easily and go on down the road—if the wind is from up the valley, that is; if it's from down the valley the leaves will pile up like snowdrifts across the drive and in front of the garage.

But even while I am mowing the grass that final time I can pause and listen to those geese with a clear conscience. And we can take off and wander whenever October beckons. I don't know where we will go, and it doesn't much matter as long as we stay out where there are more trees than people. This is the time of year when there's not even any question about the importance of trees. They declare it and you have to admit it. So we shall go and become a part of this incredibly beautiful, bountiful world that is so hospitable to man right now. And so seemingly proud of itself, so lavish in its riches. I know this is one of those high-flown figures of speech, but that's the feeling I get when I am in the midst of the October world. The gold of the sugar maples along our own stretch of road makes the pirate hoards of the Spanish Main seem like small change. And who can match the rubies and topazes and amethysts and fire opals in any swamp or on any brushy hillside?

We are going to revel in this magnificence, and I

haven't the slightest doubt that we will soon be suffused in feelings that are so full of sentiment that we will be accused of gushing like an awe-struck neophite. But October does that to one with any sensibility. Smooth old words and phrases take on at least some of their original contours and meaning, once you get out among the rocks and rills, the woods and templed hills in the blue and golden days of October. You find that, after all, this is the land that you love, and for cause. You love it and respect it and appreciate the privilege of just being here, sentient and alive.

Did you ever drive down the Blue Ridge in October and see the whole Shenandoah Valley in autumn color? Or cross the Alleghenies in Pennsylvania, on one of the old roads, not a turnpike or a superhighway, and see the vast stretch of America out there to the west, far beyond the eye's reach, beyond the Mississippi, beyond the High Plains, beyond the Rockies and the Sierra? Did you ever cross the plains from Kansas City or Omaha, westward over the old short-grass buffalo range that rises from the valley of the Missouri all the way to the Front Range beyond Denver? Did you feel how those plains, in their vastness, shrink a man down to human size and yet make him proud of his manhood? Or the way the mountains lift the spirit and exalt it, somehow, make a man feel and somewhat share the majesty of mountains? Did you ever know the Great Basin, that huge saucer between the midcontinent mountains and those of the West Coast, know the deserts by moonlight and at dawn, know the rugged canyons at midday and at dusk, know the incredible strew of rocks and the raw materials of creation waiting for time to bring order and fashion some further meaning from them?

We have been there, and we may go again, if only to see those wide valleys, so vast you could hide a major city in any one of them; to see mountains that not even the bulldozers can level; to see rivers that still defy the Army Engineers, thank God. To see how the pinyon nut harvest is on the high mesas or Arizona. To see if the chickarees still jeer at man, the intruder, in upper Idaho's grass-thick stands of tamarack. To see the aspens, like molten gold, flowing down the slopes of Colorado's Sangre de Cristo mountains. To see the cedars blue with ripe berries on the New Mexico hillsides.

We may go again. Or we may go only a day's journey from home, to see how the harvest that man has no part in whatever has literally covered the earth with its bounty, even here in this long-settled land that is called New England. Full of people, eleven million of them in six states that combined are still smaller than Nebraska; jammed with people, we so often think and say, and yet a land of woods and stony hills and upland pastures and mountains famous chiefly for their ski runs, a land where you can lose yourself in the hemlock thickets or the blueberry tangles less than a mile off the throughways. And every valley, every hillside, every bogland and swampy hollow full of color, full of nuts and red and yellow leaves and ripe pods and prickly seeds and the silk and gossamer of milkweed and thistle; more brilliant than the sunsets, more fertile with life hoarded in seed and bud than the insect hordes that feast and fertilize and gnaw and decimate the stem, the leaf, the blossom from May till sharp November. Fruitful, overflowing, bountiful beyond reckoning, for every living thing on earth. Even for man, if he would stop trying to manage and remake everything in sight except himself.

We may go only a few hours from home. We could even stay right here and still see most of these things. I could go out in the upper pasture and sit for an hour, and I would be in the very midst of the bounty, the beauty, the wholeness that makes the year complete without cutting it off from yesterday or tomorrow. All I would have to do would be to lift my face to the sky, that incredibly blue sky of a perfect October day, and open the pores of my understanding. The maples are like sunrise, and the oaks are like a stormy sky at dusk, and the ash trees that line the lower fencerow are almost as blue as the sky itself. The pasture grasses are still green, but the thistleheads are being ragged out into glistening clouds by the goldfinches. The squirrels have harvested the hickory nuts and the butternuts, leaving heaps of hulls as evidence of the plenty. The chipmunks have their granaries stocked and sit in the sun, even as I do, contemplating this marvelous world, this world of wealth in which to share. The crows proclaim their sovereignty, now that the flickers and kingbirds are gone, and the jays scream dissent at a distance. And overhead is, or soon will be, the gabble of geese.

I could stay, but the geese and my heart say go. Go,

and see the truth of October, know the enduring reality of this land that I love. So we probably shall go, if only so we can chant, eventually, with the old Navaho singers, "Beauty all around me, with it I return. Now on the trail of beauty, there I return."

1968—WINTER

The Visions and the Dreams

WE PASSED the winter solstice safely, we observed the holy days with rites and ancient ritual, and we have summed up our sins for our consciences and our profits and losses for the tax collector. When I looked last night the moon, almost full, was right where it should be and the stars not overwhelmed by moonlight were in their accustomed places. This morning the sun rose far off there in the east-southeast at a quarter after seven. Fundamental matters are pretty well in order. Only the affairs of man have been in such a state that Thanksgiving, the way we heard it, was a widespread occasion for gratitude that the nation, and the world, had survived public tumult, political turmoil and moral disintegration without total disaster.

So here we stand at the foot of the seasonal hill we call autumn, in a fairly tranquil valley of time, facing the slow climb up the cold, icy slope toward the vernal equinox and spring. Facing winter, in a word.

And here in the literal hills, more or less secure in our homes and our persons, we are thinking primarily about the weather. Not the political or economic or moral climate, but the honest-to-God, day-to-day, sun-snow-and-wind weather. . . .

I was about to apologize for that, but I can't, in all honesty. I actually wrote three manuscript pages of apologetic explanation, and I have thrown them away simply because they didn't make sense. I have heard the lamentations of the sad prophets and the morbid diagnosticians who have been so busy analyzing society and looking at the entrails of the cities. And I still know that the weather is more important ultimately than any report on the revolt of the young, the arrogance of the old or the sickness of the cities. It is no new pattern of human or municipal behavior that the jeremiads describe so graphically. Long ago the Biblical prophet, Joel, said, "Your old men shall dream dreams, your young men shall see visions." And the cities have been sick and in trouble all the way back to Sodom and Gomorrah, by the records. It is good to hear that someone is concerned about these matters, but not even a ukase from Washington can bring me to confession and penance for the sins and weaknesses of all mankind. I have enough of my own to account for. Besides, if things were really as bad as the doom-criers say, it would be my job to stay right here, keep my head, make my compromises with the weather, and be ready to help start things all over again when the time comes. So no apologies.

The basic thing that so many of the prophets keep forgetting is rhythm, the cycles. That, and the fact that change is the one constant. If they hadn't alienated themselves from the land they would know these things almost by instinct. Every villager still knows them. Things keep repeating themselves, always with some variation. Something like sunspots, which occur in complex cycles and seem to affect weather and plant growth and animal populations. Like weather itself, which is definitely cyclic.

Right here in Weatogue Valley it has happened over and over. Our weather, and a good deal of the human action and reaction, varies in cycles. I could trace it back a couple hundred years, to first settlement and land-clearing, to the iron furnaces and charcoal-burning, to lumbering, to westward migration of the younger generation, to mechanized farming, to dairying and small industry. I will go back only ten years, instead, to 1958, when we were in the midst of a wet phase of the weather cycle. Springs bubbled on the hillsides, brooks chattered across meadow and pasture all summer, hay grew tall and corn produced 150 bushels and more to the acre.

Then the weather cycle changed. The rains slackened, the snowfall dwindled, not overnight but over a few years. We came to a time of drouth. Springs dried up, wells failed, brooks ran dry in June and didn't flow again till the equinoctial rains in September. Upland pastures became dusty weed patches. Hay crops were short. To eke out the hay, dairymen increased their acreage of silo corn and almost stopped growing ear corn. Some farmers, mostly the older ones, quit and moved off the land. Younger farmers changed their methods, learned to live with the drouth, dug wells when springs failed, culled herds, got more milk from fewer cows.

We lived with the drouth almost six years. Then last year the weather began to change again. We got rain when we needed it. Crops throve. Harvests were good. This year was even better, with so much rain in June there was trouble getting the early cutting of hay in. But it was got in, one way and another. Barns bulged with it. Meanwhile, the silage corn grew eight and nine feet tall and was so laden with big ears that we shuddered to think what would happen if we got the tail end of a hurricane or even an end-of-summer gale. We got neither, and when the choppers and trucks moved into the fields there was more than the silos could hold. In field after field, the last quarter or fifth of the corn was left standing to ripen into ear corn. Now that has been picked and corn cribs that had been empty since the drouth began are full again.

Back in October I stopped to pass the time of day with a neighbor whose farm has been in the family for three generations, and he said, "I don't know what to do next year. I've got enough feed now to last me two years. I don't really have to plant an acre next spring."

"Going to take a year off?" I asked.

He shook his head and smiled. "If I took a year off and let these fields go back to weeds and brush, my dad and my grandfather would climb right out of their graves." Then he glanced at his silos and at his full corn house, as he calls it, and he said, "Come January and snow up to here, I'll be glad I've got a plenty. It's a good feeling. But come April, I'll be out plowing and planting, as usual. You can't waste a season."

And there was the substance of something you can't touch with cynicism or mockery, something you can't destroy with economic theories—the human inheritance, the love and respect for the land. Hearing it put into those words—"You can't waste a season"—I wondered again how Mississippi's Senator Eastland can face himself in the mirror after he has collected $200,000 a year for not farming his own fields; how *all* those "corporation farmers" who collect such booty can live with themselves.

But there is a difference in the whole cast of life, the fundamentals, between those who live close to the land and those who don't. I can find no better word for it than alienation—not only of the young but of all ages—of those who have been sold the idea that all our tomorrows will be paved with blacktop and managed by the technicians. It is a tragic alienation because all our yesterdays, our todays and all our tomorrows are strung on the same cord of conditions that can't be much altered if we are to go on living. Basic to those conditions are the earth, the air, and the water. Alienate yourself from these and you have lost all basis for understanding life itself.

Perhaps I should have been amused rather than appalled a few weeks ago when an art gallery in New York put on an exhibition that it called "Earthworks." It consisted of rocks, a box of humus with earthworms in it, and a 1,200-pound heap of dirt and peat moss shaped in a pile by one Robert Morris, who was listed as a sculptor. Asked what it meant, Morris leaned on his shovel and said, "This is all a part of moving out into the world." Art, modern art, having discovered the soup can and the psychedelic ego, at last had discovered the earth!

If the "Earthworks" artists, as I understand they call themselves, would only take a bus to the end of the line and walk a hundred yards, they would discover what it is like not only to move out into the world, but to live there. Right now they would discover some of the most beautiful plastic material, shaped into the most beautiful forms, any human being ever saw. We call it snow, and we welcome winter storms because they bring snow and wind to shape it. Not in a gallery or a studio, but all over the outdoors. A few weeks ago they might have seen this valley encrusted with hoar frost. Such frost, of course, is even more ephemeral than the snowdrifts; you have to get up by sunrise to see it. But that is a part of its beauty, for it is really nothing more than mist made magic by the frosty air and it becomes mist again with the puff of a warm breath. And any time this winter when there is snow in the air, they can see the incredible beauty and the unbelievable variety in snowflakes.

If one must be more down-to-earth, I suggest such commonplace things as a grove of white pines under snow, each branch a special free-form of massed crystal. Or the empty flower head of the dead thistle-stalk beside my woodshed, filled and spangled on every thorn with newfallen snow. Or the sugar maples along our road after a wet, wind-driven snow, each twig and bough and branch outlined in crystalline white against the icy-green sky at early sundown.

That is what happens on this good earth in December and January and February, and often in March. In winter, which comes every year in the endless cycle of the years. We see it happen. We live with it. It is a part of our consciousness and it is so deep in our unconscious that we know without stopping to argue it out that life itself is cyclic, and thought, and fashion, and even the trends of human behavior. The comparison of life to the year, the springtime of youth and the hoary winter of old age, is just a bit too glib, but it is not really false. There are the rhythms, the cycles, the way life and all things else change, coming around to likenesses time and again but never coming to quite the same ever again.

So there are the dreams, and there are the visions. There is summer, there is winter. There is growth, and ripeness, and rest and growth again. There are consequences, always. And all the science, all the technology, all the autoclaves and cyclotrons and computers, all the assertion or denial or proclamation, cannot change these matters or materially alter their sequence. It is the consequences that rise most often to plague us, the consequences of attempts to change the fundamentals. As with synthetic foods. The technicians tell us we could do without farms and growing crops. They could feed us on algae, or proteins from petroleum, or recovered wastes. But they forget a consequence, as so often they do. They forget a phase in the eternal cycle of the green leaf, that inconsequential blade of grass that they would cover with their highways and airports and parking lots. Without that green leaf and its whole process of photosynthesis, where would the oxygen for our gasping lungs come from?

There are visions, and there are dreams to temper them. And we are an impatient breed of animal, wanting, forever wanting, something other, something different. Trapping ourselves, not finding the door that leads to freedom, not grasping freedom when we see it. And there is the hurt that cannot be suffered longer.

Looking back through my journal for the facts of the weather ten years ago I found a story that is like a footnote to the headlines of last summer. One bright June day in 1958 a woman with haunted eyes came up our road and parked her car and came to the door. She had read a book of mine about this valley and had come up here from the city, "to see if it was real." We sat on the porch, the three of us, and she talked and Barbara and I listened. She was the wife of a prosperous broker and had, as they say, everything. She felt she had nothing, no values, no reality. She was driven almost to desperation by pressures and empty futilities. She wished she could move to the country, feel the strength and the foreverness of the land; but it was, she said, impossible—husband, children, friends, the whole net of commitments and responsibilities.

She talked and relaxed somewhat, and she went to a nearby inn and spent the night. The next morning she phoned to say she was going back, now she could take life again. At Christmas we had a card from her: "It must be magnificent there now!" The next summer a short note, leading to two questions: "Are you still there? Is it still real?" We assured her that we were and it was. Then no word until the next summer, and a single sentence: "It all seems more than ever impossible." A few days later we read her obituary in the daily paper. She was only forty-three.

No apologies, I said, and no apologies even for such a grim story of a tragic search. This is year-end and year's-beginning, and it is an old human habit to face realities when the totting up is done. . . . This is a cold morning, and there is a spit of snow in the air. The weather forecast was not encouraging, if you want mild temperatures and sunshine. The headlines in the morning's news had as dour an aspect as the weather. And yet, as I sit here and try to set it down the way it is I can't despair. There is the tangling network of commitments and responsibilities, and there is the temptation to despair over the blindness and blunderings of mankind. But there is the past, with its greatness and its glories, as well as its long, dismal eras. There is that about which to dream as well as the lure of visions. And forever and ever there is change, the one constant.

Here we are, in the homeland, the cherished soil of our inheritance. It is winter, and it will be spring again. We have known other winters, and we have learned to shelter ourselves and last out the storms. There are places where winter has no identity, where spring is not so much a season as relief from a cold in the chest. But there is also *here,* and every valley where grass still grows and every hill where trees still whisper in the moonlit breeze. There is the remembered place, still here, still real, and all the urban prophets, all the sociologists lost in the crowds, all the technologists who can't see the moonlight for the moon, can't destroy it. They can't even forget it. The grass grows even through the cracks in their paved parking yards and jet-ports. The wild daisy grows in the rubble of their sick slums. The tree spreads its roots under their interminable trash heaps and in the filthy banks of their filthy rivers.

Here we are, waiting, watching the weather, knowing all things change, seeing change every day of our lives. Seeing where the stars stand, when the moon rises, how the sun sets, clear or in a flame of clouds. Knowing, as well as we know right from wrong, that you can't waste a season. Not even winter.